ANGELS

ANGELS

OSCAR W. MCCONKIE

Deseret Book Company
Salt Lake City, Utah

CONTENTS

INTRODUCTION

Characteristic skepticism of our age has been directed against a belief in angels.

In the Old Testament and the New Testament, as well in the Book of Mormon, the Doctrine and Covenants, and the Pearl of Great Price, angelic visitations are recorded by name and by reference in the performance of God's will. As a result of scriptural exegesis, angels become a fundamental topic for both Jewish and Christian theologians. They figure in such great Judeo-Christian poetry as the *Divine Comedy* of Dante, *Paradise Lost* by Milton, *Canterbury Tales* by Chaucer, and Goethe's *Faust*.

In an attempt to discredit medieval theologians, someone characterized them as being concerned with the question as to how many angels would be able to stand on a needle's point. If any such query were ever made, it is evidence of a mistaken concept with reference to how an incorporeal substance occupies space. This and like questions were seriously discussed by such notable philosophers as Aristotle, Plato, Hobbes, and Locke.

Whether angels exist or not is a genuine issue—so much so, in my judgment, that it is a matter upon which one's salvation may be contingent.

This essay is concerned with angels. What or who are angels? What are their functions and purposes? What is their ministry? Is there rank or precedence among them? And what has all this to do with us?

God, angels,
and men
are of
the same
race

WHAT OR WHO ARE ANGELS?

No less a personage than our Lord has called our attention to angels. When Jesus' disciples asked him to "declare unto us the parable of the tares of the field," he responded: "He that soweth the good seed is the Son of Man; the field is the world . . . and the reapers are the angels" (Matthew 13:36–39). The Son of Man was and is real. He exists. The world was and is real. It has place and substance. As the Lord said, angels are real too. They are beings. They exist.

Jesus taught much about angels. He tells us what brings them joy. "Likewise, I say unto you, there is joy in the presence of the angels of God over one sinner that repenteth" (Luke 15:10). In requiring us to become as little children in our faith, he reminds us that "in heaven their angels do always behold the face of my Father. . . ." (Matthew 18:10). And in the last days he says they shall have to do with our very salvation. For, he says, he "shall send his angels . . . and they shall gather together his elect from the four winds. . . ." (Matthew 24:31).

Clearly the Lord believes in and has to do with angels. Just as clearly, judging from his holy writ, he wants us to do the same.

THE BEGINNING OF ANGELS

Let us consider the scriptures and what they have to say about angels.

First, in logical sequence, who created the angels? The apostle Paul tells us they were created by God.

For by him were all things created, that are in heaven and that are in earth, visible and invisible, whether they be thrones, or dominions, or principalities, or powers: all things were created by, and for him:

And he is before all things, and by him all things consist. (Colossians 1:16–17.)

Thus we discern that it is a scriptural doctrine that God created the angels.

Is any light shed therein as to the means of creation? Yes. When the Lord answered Job out of the whirlwind, he brought Job's attention to before the world was. He asked: "Where wast thou when I laid the foundations of the earth?" (Job 38:4). Having there established a point in time prior to the creation of the earth, the Lord spoke of the sons of God: "When the morning stars sang together, and all the sons of God shouted for joy" (Job 38:7). There were beings, referred to as "sons of God," before the creation of the earth.

In the Epistle of Paul to the Ephesians is captured the spirit of this truth as the Apostle records, ". . . I bow my knees unto the Father of our Lord Jesus Christ, of whom the whole family in heaven . . . is named. . . ." (Ephesians 3:14–15). There was a family in heaven, and it existed before the earth was made.

Both Old and New Testament citations substantiate this premise. In the Old Testament the prophet Jeremiah records the circumstances of his call to the ministry. In simple terms he tells how God called him and "put my words in thy mouth." (Jeremiah 1:9.) God told Jeremiah that he knew him in a pre-earth existence and further that he ordained Jeremiah to be a prophet before he was born on the earth. As Jeremiah records it:

Then the word of the Lord came unto me, saying,
Before I formed thee in the belly I knew thee; and before thou camest forth out of the womb I sanctified thee, and I ordained thee a prophet unto the nations. (Jeremiah 1:4–5.)

The New Testament disciples of Jesus were familiar with the scriptural concept of pre-earth sonship to God. A careful reading of an incident in our Lord's earthy ministry leaves no other valid interpretation.

> And as Jesus passed by, he saw a man which was blind from his birth.
> And his disciples asked him, saying, Master, who did sin, this man, or his parents, that he was born blind?
> Jesus answered, Neither hath this man sinned, nor his parents. . . . (John 9:1–3.)

The subject man was born blind. How could he have sinned except in a pre-earth existence? These disciples understood that the spirit within this blind man had an existence before it was tabernacled in the flesh. They knew that such spirit had opportunity to sin in such an existence, indicating that it was an accountable being at this stage of its life. The Lord assented to the assumption implicit in the query and answered that the man's blindness from birth was not caused by his actions before he was born.

The chief Apostle, Peter, makes reference to this concept and adds emphasis to the idea that our characteristics at birth are in compensation for our actions in a pre-earth life estate, saying that some persons are "elect according to the foreknowledge of God the Father" (1 Peter 1:2).

Alma says that the principle that applied to Jeremiah and the elect has general applicability to all those who are called to hold the Melchizedek Priesthood. In a discourse on the "high priesthood being after the order of his son, which order was from the foundation of the world" (Alma 13:7), he says that persons were ordained to priestly callings before they were born.

> And this is the manner after which they were ordained—being called and prepared from the foundation of the world according to the foreknowledge of God, on account of their exceeding faith and good works. (Alma 13:3.)

Ancient scripture, made new to us by revelation to the Prophet Joseph Smith, teaches that there were organized spirit personages before the physical creation of the earth. "For I, the

Lord God, created all things . . . spiritually, before they were naturally upon the face of the earth. . . . for in heaven created I them. . . . all things were before created; but spiritually were they created and made according to my word" (Moses 3:5,7).

In like manner we learn considerable detail from a great vision originally recorded by Abraham. Of "our Father which art in heaven" (Matthew 6:9), the "whole family in heaven" (Ephesians 3:15), and "the sons of God" (Job 38:7), Abraham records the following:

> Now the Lord had shown unto me, Abraham, the intelligences that were organized before the world was; and among all these there were many of the noble and great ones;
>
> And God saw these souls that they were good, and he stood in the midst of them, and he said: These I will make my rulers; for he stood among those that were spirits, and he saw that they were good; and he said unto me: Abraham, thou art one of them; thou wast chosen before thou wast born.
>
> And there stood one among them that was like unto God, and he said unto those who were with him: We will go down, for there is space there, and we will take of these materials, and we will make an earth whereon these may dwell;
>
> And we will prove them herewith, to see if they will do all things whatsoever the Lord their God shall command them;
>
> And they who keep their first estate shall be added upon; and they who keep not their first estate shall not have glory in the same kingdom with those who keep their first estate; and they who keep their second estate shall have glory added upon their heads for ever and ever. (Abraham 3:22–26.)

A modern Apostle helps us capture the meaning of Abraham's vision.

> Abraham used the name *intelligences* to apply to the spirit children of the Eternal Father. The intelligence or spirit element became intelligences after the spirits were born as individual entities. (Abra. 3:22–24.) Use of this name designates both the primal element from which the spirit offspring were created and also their inherited capacity to grow in grace, knowledge, power, and intelligence itself. . . . (Bruce R. McConkie, *Mormon Doctrine* [1966], 387.)

In the literal sense, the expression *spirit birth* has reference
to the birth of the spirit in pre-existence. Spirits are actually
born as the offspring of a Heavenly Father, a glorified and
exalted Man. (Ibid., 750.)

Brigham Young explained it this way: "Things were first created spiritually; the Father actually begat the spirits, and they
were brought forth and lived with Him." (*Journal of Discourses*,
4:218.)

Men and angels are the offspring of God. They were born to
him in a pre-earth existence. God, angels, and men are of the
same race. (Ibid., p. 217.) The angels are children of the Father
in heaven. "Because angels are of the same race as man and God,
it is with perfect logic that in the pure language spoken by Adam,
they were designated as *Anglo-man.*" (McConkie, *Mormon
Doctrine*, 37.)

As the essay continues, we shall view these other children in
their several stages of progression and retrogression.

In talking about resurrected persons, "children of the resurrection," Jesus equates the angels and the children of God. The
faithful scribe, Luke, records: "For they are equal unto the angels;
and are the children of God" (Luke 20:36).

FORM OF ANGELS

The spirit form and appearance are similar to the temporal form
or appearance. This is true of each particular form of life. The
Prophet Joseph Smith explained this principle by saying: "That
which is temporal in the likeness of that which is spiritual; the
spirit of man in the likeness of his person, as also the spirit of the
beast, and every other creature which God created" (D&C 77:2).
Thus in pre-earth life God's creations appeared somewhat as they
appear in the flesh.

The brother of Jared was accorded the singular privilege of
seeing the Lord two millennia prior to his earthly ministry. In
introducing himself, the Lord said, "Behold, I am he who was prepared from the foundation of the world to redeem my people.
Behold, I am Jesus Christ" (Ether 3:14). Then the Lord told his

beholder, "Seest thou that ye are created after mine own image? Yea, even all men were created in the beginning after mine own image" (Ether 3:15). Then the Lord told him what spirits look like before they are clothed in flesh. Their fleshy temples are after the similitude of the spirit. "Behold, this body, which ye now behold, is the body of my spirit; and man have I created after the body of my spirit; and even as I appear unto thee to be in the spirit will I appear unto my people in the flesh" (Ether 3:16).

As they have appeared throughout the ages, angels are in form like man. The most universally accepted accounts of such appearances are biblical.

When Abraham entertained three angels on the plains of Mamre, it is recorded, "He lift up his eyes and looked, and, lo, three men stood by him" (Genesis 18:2). Of the two angels (Genesis 19:1) who visited Lot's home in Sodom, the local residents inquired, "Where are the men which came in to thee this night?" (Genesis 19:5).

Daniel described Gabriel as he came to him as being in the form of man, "Behold, there stood before me as the appearance of a man" (Daniel 8:15).

All four Gospel accounts of the women at the sepulchre of the risen Lord describe "the angel of the Lord descended from heaven" (Matthew 28:2) as being in the form of a man. "They saw a young man sitting on the right side, clothed in a long white garment" (Mark 16:5). In the Gospel of John the women were described as seeing two angels (see John 20:12). Luke records the same instance: "Two men stood by them in shining garments" (Luke 24:4). Although in form like men, there was a glory that attended this angel: "His countenance was like lightning, and his raiment white as snow" (Matthew 28:3).

The most detailed description of an angel ever recorded was written by Joseph Smith. It is a description of the appearance of the angel Moroni. Here is the Prophet's witness:

> While I was thus in the act of calling upon God, I discovered a light appearing in my room, which continued to increase

until the room was lighter than at noonday, when immediately a personage appeared at my bedside, standing in the air, for his feet did not touch the floor.

He had on a loose robe of most exquisite whiteness. It was a whiteness beyond anything earthly I had ever seen; nor do I believe that any earthly thing could be made to appear so exceedingly white and brilliant. His hands were naked, and his arms also, a little above the wrist; so, also, were his feet naked, as were his legs, a little above the ankles. His head and neck were also bare. I could discover that he had no other clothing on but this robe, as it was open, so that I could see into his bosom.

Not only was his robe exceedingly white, but his whole person was glorious beyond description, and his countenance truly like lightning. The room was exceedingly light, but not so very bright as immediately around his person. When I first looked upon him, I was afraid; but the fear soon left me.

He called me by name, and said unto me that he was a messenger sent from the presence of God to me, and that his name was Moroni; that God had a work for me to do; and that my name should be had for good and evil among all nations, kindreds, and tongues, or that it should be both good and evil spoken of among all people. . . .

After this communication, I saw the light in the room begin to gather immediately around the person of him who had been speaking to me, and it continued to do so until the room was again left dark, except just around him; when, instantly I saw, as it were, a conduit open right up into heaven, and he ascended till he entirely disappeared, and the room was left as it had been before this heavenly light had made its appearance. (Joseph Smith–History 1:30–33, 43.)

This vision was repeated three times during that night, and Joseph Smith himself wrote the first-hand account thereof.

NATURE OF ANGELS

From those who have had to do with angels we can learn some things as to the nature of angels. For instance, the inspired psalmist wrote: "What is man, that thou art mindful of him? and the Son of man, that thou visitest him? For thou has made him a little lower than the angels, and hast crowned him with glory and honour" (Psalm 8:4–5). From this we may conclude that the natures of men and angels are somewhat similar. Holy writ gives us some specifics.

Some angels are holy. This is an attribute of their nature. We are indebted to the Lord for this bit of knowledge about angels. He said: "When the Son of man shall come in his glory, and all the holy angels with him, then shall he sit upon the throne of his glory" (Matthew 25:31). And again: "Whosoever therefore shall be ashamed of me and my words in this adulterous and sinful generation; of him also shall the Son of man be ashamed, when he cometh in the glory of his Father with the holy angels" (Mark 8:38).

As children of the Eternal Father, angels inherit immortality. They lived before this earth life, and they will continue to live, as personal identities, after it. The fact that angels are immortal was made clear by the Master. In explaining the Resurrection, he said: "Neither can they die any more: for they are equal unto the angels; and are the children of God, being the children of the resurrection" (Luke 20:36).

An angel rolled back the stone at the sepulchre of Jesus (see Matthew 28:2). Angels stand as witnesses to the fundamental truth of the gospel. They are perfect teachers of the plan of salvation. " . . . he doth visit us by his angels, that the plan of salvation might be made known unto us" (Alma 24:14).

The gospel is preached by those who have the "Holy Ghost sent down from heaven; which things the angels desire to look into" (1 Peter 1:12). Indeed, it is written that "angels speak by the power of the Holy Ghost" (2 Nephi 32:3).

We thus see that angels possess great knowledge. And, as with man and God, knowledge is an attribute of their nature. Some of the knowledge comes from eye witness and some from witness of the Spirit. In this, they are like holy men of God.

As with men, angels do not have a perfect knowledge of all things. They are not as God, being perfect in the attributes of their nature. The Lord himself demonstrates a limitation as to an angel's knowledge. Speaking of his second coming, the Lord says: "Heaven and earth shall pass away, but my words shall not pass away. But of that day and hour knoweth no man, no, not the angels of heaven, but my Father only" (Matthew 24:35–36). Angels do not know all things.

All beings who live the commandments are entitled to the spiritual gift of joy. It is written of men that "the Spirit of the Lord came upon them, and they were filled with joy" (Mosiah 4:3).

The angels rejoice in righteous works. They have joy when one of God's children accepts the gospel. "I say unto you, there is joy in the presence of the angels of God over one sinner that repenteth" (Luke 15:10).

Exaltation is to obtain a fulness of joy, and a fulness of joy is found only where the spirit and body are permanently reunited in exalted form (see D&C 93:33). We shall see that some angels have a fulness of joy and some do not. Men and angels have a potential of ultimate joy.

Faithful Job recorded: "Behold, he put no trust in his servants; and his angels he charged with folly" (Job 4:18). Peter tells us of "angels that sinned" and were "cast . . . down to hell" (2 Peter 2:4). It has been heretofore suggested that it is the nature of some angels to be holy (see Matthew 25:31, Mark 8:38). The foregoing biblical citations indicate that it is the nature of some angels to be bad. We shall hereafter consider each in more detail under the subtitle fallen angels.

All angels are subject to Christ and his power. Peter authoritatively declares this: " . . . Jesus Christ . . . who is gone into heaven, and is on the right hand of God; angels and authorities and powers being made subject unto him" (1 Peter 3:21–22).

During his earthly ministry our Lord demonstrated commanding authority over evil spirits: "For he said unto him, Come out of the man, thou unclean spirit. . . . And all the devils besought him, saying, Send us into the swine. . . . Jesus gave them leave. And the unclean spirits went out, and entered into the swine" (Mark 5:8, 12–13). All creatures are subject unto the Lord.

Angels, except where righteous holy men are designated as angels, do not live on the earth nor on a planet like earth. Rather, they reside in the presence of God.

> The angels do not reside on a planet like this earth;
> But they reside in the presence of God, on a globe like a sea of glass and fire, where all things for their glory are manifest, past, present, and future, and are continually before the Lord. (D&C 130:6–7.)

Angels are indeed favored beings. They may have revealed to them most things—past, present, and future. To be continually in the presence of the Lord is a superlative blessing. We should believe in and reverence them.

SOME ANGELS TO BE EXALTED, SOME NOT

As with all of our Father's children, the law of compensation applies to the angels. With reference to all of us, and all other beings created by God, we are to be tested and proved to see if we will do all things whatsoever the Lord our God shall command us (see Abraham 3:25). Those of us and those angels "who keep their first estate shall be added upon; and they who keep not their first estate shall not have glory in the same kingdom with those who keep their first estate." And finally, all, including angels, "who keep their second estate shall have glory added upon their heads forever and ever" (Abraham 3:26).

It is written of the righteous angels and Saints: "And then shall the angels be crowned with the glory of his might, and the Saints shall be filled with his glory, and receive their inheritance and be made equal with him" (D&C 88:107). This means that worthy Saints and angels shall receive exaltation. They shall be like their Father. They shall be gods. "Then shall they be gods, because they have no end; therefore shall they be from everlasting to everlasting, because they continue; then shall they be above all, because all things are subject unto them. Then shall they be gods, because they have all power . . ." (D&C 132:20). Thus is accomplished the very work and glory of the Eternal

Father—to have his children be like him (see Moses 1:39). The early Apostles taught this doctrine. " . . . Christ Jesus: Who, being in the form of God, thought it not robbery to be equal with God" (Philippians 2:5–6). "Now are we the sons of God. . . . When he shall appear, we shall be like him" (1 John 3:2).

However, there will be some angels and some Saints and some others who will not abide in the fulness of the gospel law. They shall, after their resurrection, continue as angels of God forever and ever. "For these angels did not abide my law; therefore, they cannot be enlarged, but remain separately and singly, without exaltation, in their saved condition, to all eternity; and from henceforth are not gods, but are angels of God forever and ever" (D&C 132:17). Such groups shall be "ministering servants, to minister for those who are worthy of a far more, and an exceeding, and an eternal weight of glory" (D&C 132:16).

The angels
who visit the earth
are persons who
have been assigned
to this earth

TYPES AND KINDS OF ANGELS

The angels who visit this earth are persons who have been assigned to this earth. That is, spirit children of the Eternal Father who are assigned to other earths and spheres will not minister to the inhabitants here. The Prophet Joseph Smith instructed us in this, saying, "There are no angels who minister to this earth but those who do belong or have belonged to it" (D&C 130:5). All are the children of God in various stages of progressing to become like him. The ones we know have to do with this earth.

From perusal of holy writ, one can discern several types and kinds of persons, in various stages of progression, who the Lord has used as angels in varying circumstances.

PREEXISTENT SPIRITS

We have heretofore examined scriptural evidence showing that men and angels existed as conscious identities before man was first placed on earth. We shall refer to this premortal existence as preexistence, and to those who live there as spirits. All this is made known in Abraham's great vision (see Abraham 3). John the Revelator speaks of the spirit children of the Father at this stage of our existence as angels (see Revelation 12:7–9). Abraham, Moses, Isaiah, and John detail some of our activities at this point in time.

Our having been born to and nurtured by the Eternal Father, it was determined that an earth would be made whereon we

might dwell (see Abraham 3:24). Life here was to be a probationary estate designed to prove us (see Abraham 3:25). All of
this was according to the Father's plan for the salvation of his
children (see Moses 4:2). Satan, one of the preeminent among
the angelic hosts there, sought to change the Father's plan. He
proposed "that one soul shall not be lost" (Moses 4:1). He, not
the Father, was to get the credit, "And surely I will do it; wherefore give me thine honor" (ibid.).

The Father's plan was advocated among the angels by "my
Beloved Son, which was my Beloved and Chosen from the beginning" (Moses 4:2). His was a plan allowing free choice, whereas
Satan "sought to destroy the agency of man" (Moses 4:3). Satan
rebelled and aspired to the throne of God.

There was war in heaven among the preexistent spirits.
"Michael and his angels fought against the dragon; and the dragon fought and his angels" (Revelation 12:7). And God "caused
that he should be cast down; and he became Satan . . . the devil"
(Moses 4:3–4). Thus, it was written that Satan "was angry, and
kept not his first estate; and, at that day, many followed after him"
(Abraham 3:28). These angels are said to be cast out. In the
words of Peter, "God spared not the angels that sinned, but cast
them down to hell" (2 Peter 2:4).

Active progression and retrogression took place in our first
estate. There was division among the angels. There were good
angels and there were bad angels. More will be said of the fallen
angels subsequently.

The earthly errand of one of these preexistent angels is
clearly outlined for us. Bear in mind that when the errand took
place, Adam was the first man upon the earth. No activities in
the nature of death or translation had taken place. An angel
appeared to Adam and taught him a fundamental concept of the
gospel. The angel was a preexistent spirit. There was none other
than a preexistent spirit available for such an errand at that time.

> And after many days an angel of the Lord appeared unto
> Adam, saying: Why dost thou offer sacrifices unto the Lord?

And Adam said unto him: I know not, save the Lord commanded me.

And then the angel spake, saying: This thing is a similitude of the sacrifice of the Only Begotten of the Father, which is full of grace and truth.

Wherefore, thou shalt do all that thou doest in the name of the Son, and thou shalt repent and call upon God in the name of the Son forevermore. (Moses 5:6–8.)

One type and kind of person who has served the Lord as an angel is a spirit child of the Eternal Father known as a preexistent spirit.

TRANSLATED BEINGS

In the early days of the history of the world many righteous men were translated. That is, during the first two millennia of the earth's history, many faithful members of the Church were changed from their earthly sphere of existence to a terrestrial order. Such a change is called translation. (see Joseph Smith, *Teachings of the Prophet Joseph Smith [TPJS]* sel. Joseph Fielding Smith [1976], 170–71.) In effect, such righteous Saints were taken into the heavenly realms without tasting death. More precisely, they passed through death and "were with Christ in his resurrection, and . . . shall be in the presence of the Lamb" (D&C 133:55). This amounted to an instantaneous death and resurrection at that time.

Persons who were translated after the resurrection of Jesus will pass through death at the second coming of Christ when they "shall be changed in the twinkling of an eye" from mortality to immortality (D&C 43:32). Pending the Second Coming, translated persons minister according to God's purposes.

Enoch and his people were translated. The city of Enoch was a populous city. The translation of these people took place shortly after Adam's death (See Moses 7:18–21, 31, 63, 69; D&C 38:4; 45:11–14; 84:99–100; Genesis 5:22–24; Hebrews 11:5).

The Inspired Version of Genesis tells us of subsequent translations. Of some faithful holders of the Melchizedek Priesthood after the great flood it is recorded:

And men having this faith, coming up unto this order of God, were translated and taken up into heaven.

And now, Melchizedek was a priest of this order; therefore he obtained peace in Salem, and was called the Prince of peace.

And his people wrought righteousness, and obtained heaven, and sought for the city of Enoch which God had before taken, separating it from the earth, having reserved it unto the latter days, or the end of the world. (Inspired Version, Genesis 14:32–34.)

Moses was translated. The Old Testament account indicates he was buried by the hand of the Lord (see Deuteronomy 34:5–7). However, this figure of speech is interpreted for us in the Book of Mormon wherein is said, "the scriptures saith the Lord took Moses unto himself" (Alma 45:19).

Alma the younger was translated. Of him it is said that he "was taken up by the Spirit . . . and we suppose that he [God] has also received Alma in the spirit, unto himself" (Ibid.).

Elijah was translated. His ascent into heaven is told with a flourish. "There appeared a chariot of fire, and horses of fire, and parted them both asunder; and Elijah went up by a whirlwind into heaven" (2 Kings 2:11).

There is a reason that we have record of many translations in the earliest of times and very few translations after our Lord's earthly ministry. It was not until the meridian of time that the Lord opened the door to the preaching of the gospel to the spirits in prison (see 1 Peter 3:18–20; Moses 7:36–40). Since that time the righteous, in due course, could die and be assigned a labor in the spirit world. But what of before? There was no labor there for the righteous dead. Thus it was that many of the ancient righteous Saints were translated and given other ministries to perform pending their eventual exaltation.

The Prophet Joseph Smith says that some of the ministries to which translated beings were assigned were to be angels of God. They are "held in reserve to be ministering angels unto many planets." (*TPJS*, 170.) A biblical characterization of an angelic purpose and visitation is given us in the New Testament in the case of two translated beings, Moses and Elijah, who appeared to Peter, James, and John on the Mount of Transfiguration. "And, behold, there appeared unto them Moses and Elias talking with him. Then answered Peter, and said unto Jesus, Lord, it is good for us to be here: if thou wilt, let us make here three tabernacles; one for thee, and one for Moses, and one for Elias" (Matthew 17:3–4). This is an account of angelic administration. Modern prophets have told us why Moses and Elijah came to the chief apostle. (See *TPJS*, 158; Joseph Fielding Smith, *Doctrines of Salvation*, 2:107–111.)

> Moses and Elijah were translated so that they could come with bodies of flesh and bones to confer keys upon Peter, James, and John on the mount of transfiguration, an event destined to occur prior to the beginning of the resurrection. (McConkie, *Mormon Doctrine*, 805.)

This is an illustration of translated beings used as angels to perform God's purposes.

A few special persons who have lived in the Christian era have been translated. The most well-known among these was John. John may have been present when Jesus said, "There be some standing here, which shall not taste of death, till they see the Son of man coming in his kingdom" (Matthew 16:28). Whether present when that sentence was uttered or not, John was translated.

> Then Peter, turning about, seeth the disciple whom Jesus loved following; which also leaned on his breast at supper. . . .
>
> Jesus saith unto him, If I will that he tarry till I come, what is that to thee? follow thou me.
>
> Then went this saying abroad among the brethren, that that disciple should not die: yet Jesus said not unto him, He shall not die; but, If I will that he tarry till I come, what is that to thee? (John 21:20, 22–23.)

As Joseph Smith pondered this passage of scripture, he

inquired of the Lord whether John, the beloved disciple, tarried in the flesh or had died. He was given the following revelation.

> And the Lord said unto me: John, my beloved, what desirest thou? For if you shall ask what you will, it shall be granted unto you.
>
> And I said unto him: Lord, give unto me power over death, that I may live and bring souls unto thee.
>
> And the Lord said unto me: Verily, verily, I say unto thee, because thou desirest this thou shalt tarry until I come in my glory, and shalt prophesy before nations, kindreds, tongues and people.
>
> And for this cause the Lord said unto Peter: If I will that he tarry till I come, what is that to thee? For he desired of me that he might bring souls unto me, but thou desiredst that thou mightest speedily come unto me in my kingdom.
>
> I say unto thee, Peter, this was a good desire; but my beloved has desired that he might do more, or a greater work yet among men than what he has before done.
>
> Yea, he has undertaken a greater work; therefore I will make him as flaming fire and a ministering angel; he shall minister for those who shall be heirs of salvation who dwell on the earth.
>
> And I will make thee to minister for him and for thy brother James; and unto you three I will give this power and the keys of this ministry until I come.
>
> Verily I say unto you, ye shall both have according to your desires, for ye both joy in that which ye have desired. (D&C 7.)

Attention is drawn to the phrase "I will make him . . . a ministering angel." In partial fulfillment of this statement, this same John, in concert with Peter and James, was a ministering angel to Joseph Smith "in the wilderness between Harmony, Susquehanna county, and Colesville, Broome county, on the Susquehanna river, declaring [himself] as possessing the keys of the kingdom" (D&C 128:20). This is a further illustration of a translated being used as an angel.

On the American continent, at the time of Christ's appearance to the Nephites, three of the then chosen twelve were also given power over death so that they could continue their ministry until the second coming (see 3 Nephi 28). It is from the account of the translation of these three Nephites that we gain most of our knowledge of the present ministry of translated persons among men. The account of their selection is as follows:

> And it came to pass when Jesus had said these words, he spake unto his disciples, one by one, saying unto them: What is it that ye desire of me, after that I am gone to the Father?
>
> And they all spake, save it were three, saying: We desire that after we have lived unto the age of man, that our ministry, wherein thou hast called us, may have an end, that we may speedily come unto thee in thy kingdom.
>
> And he said unto them: Blessed are ye because ye desired this thing of me; therefore, after that ye are seventy and two years old ye shall come unto me in my kingdom; and with me ye shall find rest.
>
> And when he had spoken unto them, he turned himself unto the three, and said unto them: What will ye that I should do unto you, when I am gone unto the Father?
>
> And they sorrowed in their hearts, for they durst not speak unto him the thing which they desired.
>
> And he said unto them: Behold, I know your thoughts, and ye have desired the thing which John, my beloved, who was with me in my ministry, before that I was lifted up by the Jews, desired of me.
>
> Therefore, more blessed are ye, for ye shall never taste of death; but ye shall live to behold all the doings of the Father unto the children of men, even until all things shall be fulfilled according to the will of the Father, when I shall come in my glory with the powers of heaven.
>
> And ye shall never endure the pains of death; but when I shall come in my glory ye shall be changed in the twinkling of an eye from mortality to immortality; and then shall ye be blessed in the kingdom of my Father.
>
> And again, ye shall not have pain while ye shall dwell in the flesh, neither sorrow save it be for the sins of the world; and all this will I do because of the thing which ye have desired of me, for ye have desired that ye might bring the souls of men unto me, while the world shall stand.

And for this cause ye shall have fulness of joy; and ye shall sit down in the kingdom of my Father; yea, your joy shall be full, even as the Father hath given me fulness of joy; and ye shall be even as I am, and I am even as the Father; and the Father and I are one. (3 Nephi 28:1–10.)

From the foregoing account, it is apparent that translated beings after the resurrection of Jesus "never taste of death"; "live to behold all the doings of the Father unto . . . when I come in my glory"; "when I shall come . . . shall be changed in the twinkling of an eye from mortality to immortality"; "shall not have pain . . . neither sorrow save it be for the sins of the world"; "shall have a fulness of joy . . . in the kingdom of my Father." As the prophet Mormon spoke of these happenings, he said that these three were holy men "sanctified in the flesh" (3 Nephi 28:39).

Mormon interlineates in his recording of the Three Nephites and says: "And now I, Mormon, make an end of speaking concerning these things. . . . But behold, I have seen them, and they have ministered unto me. . . . And they are as the angels of God" (3 Nephi 28:24, 26, 30). Here, then, is the prime scriptural rendition of the use of translated beings as angels of God.

In addition, we are told that these particular angels will minister to others. They will minister to both Jew and Gentile and to scattered and lost Israel.

And behold they will be among the Gentiles, and the Gentiles shall know them not.

They will also be among the Jews, and the Jews shall know them not.

And it shall come to pass, when the Lord seeth fit in his wisdom that they shall minister unto all the scattered tribes of Israel, and unto all nations, kindreds, tongues and people, and shall bring out of them unto Jesus many souls, that their desire may be fulfilled, and also because of the convincing power of God which is in them. (3 Nephi 28:27–29.)

In the New Testament, Jude speaks of angels—preexistent angels—and angels ministering to men on earth (See Jude 1:6, 9). He then quotes a prophecy of Enoch, who, as we have observed, "was taken up into heaven" (Moses 7:21), that is, was translated. The Prophet Joseph Smith said of the translated Enoch: "He is a ministering angel, to minister to those who shall be heirs of salvation, and appeared unto Jude" (*TPJS*, 170). Here, then, is another scriptural account of a translated being, ministering as an angel.

As one contemplates these mysteries, the apostle Paul's closing chapter to the Hebrew Saints comes to mind. He counsels them to "be not forgetful to entertain strangers: for thereby some have entertained angels unawares" (Hebrews 13:2). The Lord may have had such translated persons in mind when he said in our day: "All are under sin, except those which I have reserved unto myself, holy men that ye know not of" (D&C 49:8).

SPIRITS OF JUST MEN MADE PERFECT

Most persons have died and are awaiting the day of their resurrection. Many among them will be resurrected on the morning of the first resurrection with celestial bodies of great glory. Modern scripture refers to these as "just men made perfect" (D&C 76:69). These are the spirits of men who have worked out their salvation but are awaiting the day of the Resurrection. The revelation says that these just men made perfect are part of the "innumerable company of angels" (D&C 76:67) in a heavenly place.

> These shall dwell in the presence of God and his Christ forever and ever.
>
> These are they whom he shall bring with him, when he shall come in the clouds of heaven to reign on the earth over his people.
>
> These are they who shall have part in the first resurrection.
>
> These are they who shall come forth in the resurrection of the just.
>
> These are they who are come unto Mount Zion, and unto the city of the living God, the heavenly place, the holiest of all.

These are they who have come to an innumerable company of angels, to the general assembly and church of Enoch, and of the Firstborn.

These are they whose names are written in heaven, where God and Christ are the judge of all.

These are they who are just men made perfect through Jesus the mediator of the new covenant, who wrought out this perfect atonement through the shedding of his own blood. (D&C 76:62–69.)

For the purposes of this discussion, attention is called to the phraseology that just men made perfect are angels. The spirits of certain persons who have left their bodies in death and who reside in the spirit world are angels. The spirit of Jesus ministered in the spirit world for three days before it was reunited with the body in the resurrection (see 1 Peter 3:18–21; 4:6; D&C 76:73–74). "And also they who are the spirits of men kept in prison, whom the Son visited, and preached the gospel unto them, that they might be judged according to men in the flesh" (D&C 76:73). Peter tells of this visitation:

For Christ also hath once suffered for sins, the just for the unjust, that he might bring us to God, being put to death in the flesh, but quickened by the Spirit:

By which also he went and preached unto the spirits in prison;

Which sometime were disobedient, when once the long-suffering of God waited in the days of Noah, while the ark was a preparing, wherein few, that is, eight souls were saved by water. . . .

For for this cause was the gospel preached also to them that are dead, that they might be judged according to men in the flesh, but live according to God in the spirit. (1 Peter 3:18–20; 4:6.)

In his vision of the redemption of the dead, President Joseph F. Smith saw that during his ministry to the spirits in prison, "the Lord went not in person among the wicked and the disobedient who had rejected the truth," but that he went "to declare . . . liberty to the captives" who had been faithful, to the vast assemblage of the righteous, for they "had looked upon the long absence of their spirits from their bodies as a bondage" (Joseph F. Smith, *Gospel Doctrine*, 472–75). It is to these faithful that the terminology "just men made perfect" applies.

The apostle Paul uses the same phraseology. He writes of the "innumerable company of angels" who are come to the "heavenly Jerusalem" as "the spirits of just men made perfect" (Hebrews 12:22–23). The New Testament thus equates just men made perfect to angels.

Paul writes that these angels reside in "the city of the living God" (Hebrews 12:22), or, as we would say, they live in heaven. The Prophet Joseph Smith says that "There are two kinds of beings in heaven, namely: Angels, who are resurrected person-ages, having bodies of flesh and bones—. . . Secondly: the spirits of just men made perfect, they who are not resurrected, but in-herit the same glory" (D&C 129:1, 3).

God uses the spirits of just men made perfect as angels in accomplishing his purposes. Men of spiritual maturity and sensi-tivity record many ministrations of such angels. President Wilford Woodruff recorded many such angelic visitations to him. "Joseph Smith visited me a great deal after his death, and taught me many important principles" (*The Discourses of Wilford Woodruff*, 288).

Careful consideration of some of the prominent biblical angelic visitations leads one to the conclusion that the visitants were spirits of just men made perfect. For example, the twenty-sixth and twenty-seventh verses of the first chapter of Luke com-mence what is perhaps the most well-known of all angelic visits: "The angel Gabriel was sent from God . . . to a virgin . . . and the virgin's name was Mary." Here, holy writ bears record of the activ-ities of an angel by name. We are indebted to the Prophet Joseph Smith for the insight that Gabriel is Noah (*TPJS*, 157). With this added knowledge, and knowing that no one was resurrected prior to Jesus, it follows that Gabriel was the spirit of a just man made perfect at that point in time. The same could be said of Gabriel's ministrations to Daniel (see Daniel 8:16; 9:21) and his appear-ance to Zacharias (see Luke 1:5–19).

Joseph Smith had such familiarity with angels that he tells us how to recognize the various kinds of angels. Of an angelic visitant he says:

> If he be the spirit of a just man made perfect he will come in his glory; for that is the only way he can appear—
>
> Ask him to shake hands with you, but he will not move, because it is contrary to the order of heaven for a just man to deceive; but he will still deliver his message. (D&C 129:6–7.)

The spirits of just men made perfect are used as angels in God's purposes.

RESURRECTED PERSONAGES

In fulfillment of prophecy—"And many graves shall be opened, and shall yield up many of their dead; and many Saints shall appear unto many" (Helaman 14:25)—after the resurrection of Jesus many of the righteous dead came forth from the grave.

> And, behold, the veil of the temple was rent in twain from the top to the bottom; and the earth did quake, and the rocks rent;
>
> And the graves were opened; and many bodies of the Saints which slept arose,
>
> And came out of the graves after his resurrection, and went into the holy city, and appeared unto many. (Matthew 27:51–53.)

As it was prophesied, so it came to pass. Many righteous persons were resurrected after Jesus' resurrection, and they ministered as angels to many.

Resurrected persons have "bodies of flesh and bones" (D&C 129:1). The Gospel according to Luke makes this perfectly clear:

> Jesus himself stood in the midst of them, and saith unto them, Peace be unto you.
>
> But they were terrified and affrighted, and supposed that they had seen a spirit.
>
> And he said unto them, Why are ye troubled? and why do thoughts arise in your hearts?

Behold my hands and my feet, that it is I myself: handle me, and see; for a spirit hath not flesh and bones, as ye see me have. (Luke 24:36–39; see also D&C 129:2.)

The resurrection is the creation of an immortal soul. It consists of the uniting of the body and spirit in immortality (Smith, *Doctrines of Salvation*, 2:258–301). A resurrected being is one for whom body and spirit are inseparably connected. It is a state of incorruption (see 1 Corinthians 15; Alma 11:37–46; 12:12–18).

Resurrected persons serving as angels are tangible. Modern scripture specifically designates "angels, who are resurrected personages" as "having bodies of flesh and bones" (D&C 129:1).

This type of angel has been instrumental in the restoration of the gospel in this dispensation. It was of such angels that John recorded: "And I saw another angel fly in the midst of heaven, having the everlasting gospel to preach unto them that dwell on the earth, and to every nation, and kindred, and tongue, and people" (Revelation 14:6). John saw in vision the fulness of the gospel being restored in these last days by angels.

John the Baptist was such an angel. He restored the Aaronic Priesthood to the earth as a part of the restoration of all things (see D&C 13).

Peter and James were also resurrected personages serving as angelic ministrants when they restored the Melchizedek Priesthood to the earth (see D&C 27:12–13; 128:20).

Moroni was such an angelic ministrant when he appeared to Joseph Smith and brought to the world the Book of Mormon (Joseph Smith–History 1:30–32; D&C 128:20).

Michael was such an angelic visitant when he declared his "dispensation . . . rights . . . keys . . . honors . . . glory, and . . . priesthood" (D&C 128:21) in his part of the restoration.

Gabriel, at the stage of his ministry wherein he played a part in bringing all things together in one dispensation, was a resurrected angel (ibid.). When he appeared to Mary (Luke 1:26–38), it was to tell her that she was to be the mother of the Son of God. Inasmuch as this same Son of God was the first fruits of the resurrection, Gabriel, at that time, was the spirit of a just man made perfect.

Raphael was a resurrected personage when he played the role of an angel in the restoration of all things (see D&C 128:21).

Moses, in his indispensable role in committing "the keys of the gathering of Israel . . . and the leading of the ten tribes from the land of the north" (D&C 110:11) in this dispensation, was a resurrected personage. It has been heretofore observed that when he appeared on the Mount of Transfiguration in the meridian of time, he was a translated being.

Elijah, in restoring the keys that would "turn the hearts of the fathers to the children, and the children to the fathers," appeared as a resurrected angel (D&C 110:13–16). As with Moses, his prior angelic administration on the Mount of Transfiguration had been as a translated being.

"Elias appeared, and committed the dispensation of the gospel of Abraham, saying that in us and our seed all generations after us should be blessed" (D&C 110:12). The ancient prophet was a resurrected being at this time.

For their role in the restoration of all things, Moses and Elijah, who in the first instance had been translated, "were with Christ in his resurrection" (D&C 133:55).

These are not all of the resurrected angels who had part in the restoration of the fulness of the gospel. The restoring angel, as envisioned by John, was a composite angel. That is, he represented the aforesaid angels and others. For it is written that "divers angels, from Michael or Adam down to the present time" would declare "their dispensation, their rights, their keys, their honors, their majesty and glory, and the power of their priesthood" (D&C 128:21). And so it is that the prophecy made by John has come to pass. Angels have restored the everlasting gospel.

RIGHTEOUS MORTAL MEN

The scriptures refer to certain mortal men who act as messengers or agents of God as angels. This is proper usage of the term inasmuch as angels are associated as messengers from God. Righteous holy men are thus sometimes referred to as angels.

The King James Version of the Old Testament gives an account of two angels who came to rescue Lot from Sodom. The wicked inhabitants of Sodom referred to the angels as men and sought to improperly use them (see Genesis 19). In the nineteenth chapter of Genesis in the Inspired Version, Joseph Smith indicates that these "angels of God" "were holy men."

The New Testament uses the term *angel* to designate certain church leaders. Thus, it is written: "Unto the angel of the church of Ephesus write" (Revelation 2:1). There are seven such uses of the term *angel* in the New Testament.

Once again the Prophet Joseph Smith, in the Inspired Version, sheds light on these biblical renditions of the term angel. In each instance his rendering of the passage is "the servant of the church" in lieu of "the angel of the church" (Inspired Version, Revelation 2:1; 3:1, 7, 14).

There is some evidence in the scriptures that the term *angel* may mean both heavenly personages and earthly persons. Of Jesus it is said in the last days: "And he shall send his angels with a great sound of a trumpet, and they shall gather together his elect from the four winds" (Matthew 24:31). To the Saints in our day the Lord says, "Verily, I say unto you that ye are chosen out of the world to declare my gospel with the sound of rejoicing, as with the voice of a trump. . . . And ye are called to bring to pass the gathering of mine elect; for mine elect hear my voice" (D&C 29:4, 7). Righteous Saints, engaged in missionary endeavors, are numbered with the angels the New Testament says shall gather together the elect. Heavenly angels are no doubt also engaged in this cause.

Righteous and holy mortal men may properly be designated as angels.

THE LORD AS THE ANGEL

The Lord is not an angel in the usual sense. However, Christ is the messenger of salvation and the messenger of the covenant (see Malachi 3:1). He is the one who carries out the will of the Father (see Moses 4:2). Therefore, the Lord may play the part of an angel. Although not usual, it is proper to call him an angel. Some biblical citations refer to the Lord as an angel. In point of fact, the Lord is called *The Angel* in a blessing given by Jacob. "God, before whom my fathers Abraham and Isaac did walk, the God which fed me all my life long unto this day. The Angel which redeemed me from all evil" (Genesis 48:15–16).

The King James Version of Exodus says of Moses' experience on Horeb, the mountain of God, "And the angel of the Lord appeared unto him in a flame of fire out of the midst of a bush: and he looked, and, behold, the bush burned with fire, and the bush was not consumed . . . God called unto him out of the midst of the bush, and said . . . I am the God of thy father" (Exodus 3:2, 4, 6). This is a standard biblical reference to the Lord as an angel.

Joseph Smith says this should have been rendered "the presence of the Lord appeared unto him, in a flame of fire in the midst of a bush" (Inspired Version, Exodus 3:2). Be this as it may, the standard translation calls God an angel, and attention should be called to this in an essay on the types and kinds of angels. One way that the term *angel* is used in the holy scriptures is to denote the Lord God himself.

The purposes and
functions of angels are as
many and varied
as the purposes
and functions of God

ANGELIC PURPOSES
AND FUNCTIONS

The purposes and functions of the angels are legion. They encompass substantially the whole of the purposes and functions of God. The most cogent and succinct restatement of God's purposes is given in his own words: "For behold, this is my work and my glory—to bring to pass the immortality and eternal life of man" (Moses 1:39).

Angels are a medium of revelation from God to man. They act on his errands. "For behold, the Lord God hath sent forth the angel crying through the midst of heaven, saying: Prepare ye the way of the Lord" (D&C 133:17). Holy writ is literally filled with accounts of angelic visitants doing God's bidding. Herewith are listed some of their doings.

DIVINE MESSENGERS

God's messengers are called angels. These are persons whom he sends (often from his personal presence in the eternal worlds) to deliver his messages. The most universally known angelic messenger is Gabriel. The account of his errands to Zacharias and Mary is recorded in the Gospel of Luke:

> And there appeared unto him an angel of the Lord standing on the right side of the altar of incense.
> And when Zacharias saw him, he was troubled, and fear fell upon him.

But the angel said unto him, Fear not, Zacharias: for thy prayer is heard; and thy wife Elisabeth shall bear thee a son, and thou shalt call his name John.

And thou shalt have joy and gladness; and many shall rejoice at his birth.

For he shall be great in the sight of the Lord, and shall drink neither wine nor strong drink; and he shall be filled with the Holy Ghost, even from his mother's womb.

And many of the children of Israel shall he turn to the Lord their God.

And he shall go before him in the spirit and power of Elias, to turn the hearts of the fathers to the children, and the disobedient to the wisdom of the just; to make ready a people prepared for the Lord.

And Zacharias said unto the angel, Whereby shall I know this? for I am an old man, and my wife well stricken in years.

And the angel answering said unto him, I am Gabriel, that stand in the presence of God; and am sent to speak unto thee, and to shew thee these glad tidings.

And, behold, thou shalt be dumb, and not able to speak, until the day that these things shall be performed, because thou believest not my words, which shall be fulfilled in their season.

And the people waited for Zacharias, and marvelled that he tarried so long in the temple.

And when he came out, he could not speak unto them: and they perceived that he had seen a vision in the temple: for he beckoned [continued making signs] unto them, and remained speechless.

And it came to pass, that, as soon as the days of his ministration were accomplished, he departed to his own house.

And after those days his wife Elisabeth conceived, and hid herself five months, saying,

Thus hath the Lord dealt with me in the days wherein he looked on me, to take away my reproach among men.

And in the sixth month the angel Gabriel was sent from God unto a city of Galilee, named Nazareth,

To a virgin espoused to a man whose name was Joseph, of the house of David; and the virgin's name was Mary.

And the angel came in unto her, and said, Hail, thou that art highly favoured, the Lord is with thee: blessed art thou among women.

And when she saw him, she was troubled at his saying, and cast in her mind what manner of salutation this should be.

And the angel said unto her, Fear not, Mary: for thou hast found favour with God.

And, behold, thou shalt conceive in thy womb, and bring forth a son, and shalt call his name Jesus.

He shall be great, and shall be called the Son of the Highest: and the Lord God shall give unto him the throne of his father David:

And he shall reign over the house of Jacob for ever; and of his kingdom there shall be no end.

Then said Mary unto the angel, How shall this be, seeing I know not a man?

And the angel answered and said unto her, The Holy Ghost shall come upon thee, and the power of the Highest shall overshadow thee: therefore also that holy thing which shall be born of thee shall be called the Son of God.

And, behold, thy cousin Elisabeth, she hath also conceived a son in her old age: and this is the sixth month with her, who was called barren.

For with God nothing shall be impossible [no word from God shall be void of power].

And Mary said, Behold the handmaid of the Lord; be it unto me according to thy word. And the angel departed from her. (Luke 1:11–38.)

A prominent Old Testament illustration is found in 2 Kings: "And the angel of the Lord said unto Elijah, Go down with him: be not afraid of him. And he arose, and went down with him unto the king" (2 Kings 1:15).

A less well-known illustration, but quotable to demonstrate the general use of such beings at various times and places, was recorded by the Old Testament prophet, Zechariah: "Then said I, O my Lord, what are these? And the angel that talked with me said unto me, I will shew thee what these be" (Zechariah 1:9).

And to one among the Saints in the former-day Church, "The angel of the Lord spake unto Philip, saying, Arise, and go toward the south unto the way that goeth down from Jerusalem unto Gaza, which is desert" (Acts 8:26).

Some of the words of God imparted to men by such servants

are of such significance in his plan of salvation that they are listed here separately.

TO TEACH

In the very beginning, God established a pattern of his teaching men by way of angels. It started with the first man, Adam.

> And after many days an angel of the Lord appeared unto Adam, saying: Why dost thou offer sacrifices unto the Lord? And Adam said unto him: I know not, save the Lord commanded me.
>
> And then the angel spake, saying: This thing is a similitude of the sacrifice of the Only Begotten of the Father, which is full of grace and truth.
>
> Wherefore, thou shalt do all that thou doest in the name of the Son, and thou shalt repent and call upon God in the name of the Son forevermore. (Moses 5:6–8.)

Thus the basic relationship between the Son of God and man was announced and taught by an angel. This system of teaching has been repeated over and over again.

The Book of Mormon furnishes the best examples of the use of angels as teachers. King Benjamin commences one of his great sermons by saying, "And the things which I shall tell you are made known to me by an angel from God." The angel said unto the king, "I am come to declare unto you the glad tidings of great joy" (Mosiah 3:2–3). Then is recorded one of the most significant sermons ever given, including this key: "Salvation was, and is, and is to come, in and through the atoning blood of Christ, the Lord Omnipotent" (Mosiah 3:18).

Alma tells us that "angels are declaring it unto many at this time in our land; and this is for the purpose of preparing the hearts of the children of men to receive his word" (Alma 13:24). He further records: "Many did declare unto the people that they had seen angels and had conversed with them; and thus they had told them things of God, and of his righteousness" (Alma 19:34). Alma says plainly, "Therefore, in his mercy he doth visit us by his angels, that the plan of salvation might be made known unto us as well as unto future generations" (Alma 24:14).

TO CALL MEN TO REPENTANCE

The Lord's gospel is termed "the gospel of repentance" (D&C 13). This is how important the principle of repentance is. It is not surprising, then, that Nephi tells us, "He hath sent his angels to declare the tidings of the conditions of repentance, which bringeth unto the power of the Redeemer, unto the salvation of their souls" (Helaman 5:11).

Mormon says that the calling of men to repentance is part of the ministry of angels.

> Neither have angels ceased to minister unto the children of men.
>
> For behold, they are subject unto him, to minister according to the word of his command, showing themselves unto them of strong faith and a firm mind in every form of godliness.
>
> And the office of their ministry is to call men unto repentance, and to fulfil and to do the work of the covenants of the Father. . . . (Moroni 7:29–31.)

TO TESTIFY OF THE FATHER AND THE SON

One of the fundamental purposes and functions of the angels is to bear testimony of the Father and the Son. "And Enoch beheld angels descending out of heaven, bearing testimony of the Father and Son" (Moses 7:27).

Once again, it is Mormon who is quoted as specifying testimony bearing as one of the functions of the ministry of angels: "Neither have angels ceased to minister unto the children of men. . . . And the office of their ministry is . . . that they may bear testimony of him" (Moroni 7:29, 31).

TO GUIDE MEN

One of the purposes of angels is to guide men in their performance of God's work. To Abraham, "the Lord God of heaven" said that "he shall send his angel before thee" (Genesis 24:7) to guide him in his activities.

As Moses performed God's will in liberating captive Israel, he was promised: "Behold, I send an Angel before thee, to keep thee in the way, and to bring thee into the place which I have pre-pared" (Exodus 23:20). And so it was. "And the angel of God, which went before the camp of Israel, removed . . ." (Exodus 14:19).

It was an "angel of the Lord" who guided Philip through the desert (Acts 8:26).

TO GIVE MEN PRIESTHOOD AND KEYS

In New Testament terminology, certain men are "ordained by angels" (Galatians 3:19). That is, certain priestly keys and author-ities are given to men by angels from God.

Significantly, at the commencement of the dispensation of the fulness of times, it was the Angel Moroni who told the Prophet Joseph Smith, using the words of the Lord, "I will reveal unto you the Priesthood" by way of angelic administrations (see Joseph Smith–History 1:38). The specific angelic ministrant here referred to is "Elijah the prophet" (Ephesians 1:10; D&C 2:1–3; 27:13). True to his word, this angel did take part in the restora-tion of priesthood keys of this dispensation (see D&C 110:13–16). True to the concept he enunciated, the Lord sent John the Baptist, by then a resurrected personage, to Joseph Smith and Oliver Cowdery, on 15 May 1829, to "confer the Priesthood of Aaron" (D&C 13). Subsequently, in time, he sent "Peter, James, and John in the wilderness between Harmony, Susquehanna county, and Colesville, Broome county, on the Susquehanna river, declaring themselves as possessing the keys of the kingdom, and of the dispensation of the fulness of times" (D&C 128:20). The Melchizedek Priesthood was thus restored to the earth by the angelic presence of Peter, James, and John. The Lord himself is "a priest for ever after the order of Melchisedec" (Hebrews 7:17), and he it was who had chosen and called Peter,

James, and John and "ordained" (John 15:16) them to offices in this priesthood.

There were many other angels who attended Joseph Smith in gathering "together in one all things, both which are in heaven, and which are on earth" (D&C 27:13; see also Ephesians 1:10). He records the remarkable occurrences of 3 April 1836, in the temple at Kirtland, Ohio:

> Moses appeared before us, and committed unto us the keys of the gathering of Israel from the four parts of the earth, and the leading of the ten tribes from the land of the north.
>
> After this, Elias appeared, and committed the dispensation of the gospel of Abraham, saying that in us and our seed all generations after us should be blessed.
>
> After this vision had closed, another great and glorious vision burst upon us; for Elijah the prophet, who was taken to heaven without tasting death, stood before us, and said:
>
> Behold, the time has fully come, which was spoken of by the mouth of Malachi—testifying that he [Elijah] should be sent, before the great and dreadful day of the Lord come—
>
> To turn the hearts of the fathers to the children, and the children to the fathers, lest the whole earth be smitten with a curse—
>
> Therefore, the keys of this dispensation are committed into your hands; and by this ye may know that the great and dreadful day of the Lord is near, even at the doors. (D&C 110:11–16.)

The Prophet Joseph Smith records other visitations in glorious terms: " . . . Glad tidings from Cumorah! Moroni, an angel from heaven, declaring the fulfilment of the prophets—the book to be revealed . . . And the voice of Michael, the archangel; the voice of Gabriel, and of Raphael, and of divers angels, from Michael or Adam down to the present time, all declaring their dispensation, their rights, their keys, their honors, their majesty and glory, and the power of their priesthood; giving line upon line, precept upon precept; here a little, and there a little; giving us consolation by holding forth that which is to come, confirming our hope!" (D&C 128:20–21).

Think of it! In our day the priesthood of God, with all its keys and authorities, all of its rights, majesty, and glory, has been restored by angelic administrations. And all of this according to the pattern afore set by God himself!

These are some of the most significant of all angelic functions. They are the fulfillment of many major prophecies. In some of the words and the reasoning of the apostle Paul: the gospel is "the power of God unto salvation" (Romans 1:16); God has chosen and called certain brethren and given them "the power of God: to minister and "by the foolishness of preaching to save them that believe" (1 Corinthians 1:21); "And no man taketh this honour unto himself, but he that is called of God, as was Aaron" (Hebrews 5:4). Aaron was called through revelation to the living prophet to "minister unto [God] in the priest's office" (Exodus 28:1) and was ordained and set apart as was Joshua. "And the Lord said unto Moses, Take thee Joshua the Son of Nun, a man in whom is the spirit, and lay thine hand upon him" (Numbers 27:18).

The ability to ordain and set apart legal administrators in the gospel and its ordinances by the laying on of hands was restored to the earth by the angels as described above. It is thus not an overstatement to say that our very salvation is now available because of these angelic administrations. The keys of the kingdom of heaven, with the power to bind on earth and in heaven given by Jesus to Peter (see Matthew 16:13–19), were returned to the earth by the bearer. Our salvation is contingent upon the administration of angels.

TO GATHER THE ELECT

Matthew records that in the day of the coming of the Son of Man "in the clouds of heaven with power and great glory . . . he shall send his angels with a great sound of a trumpet, and they shall gather together his elect from the four winds" (Matthew 24:30–31). Thus we conclude that one of the functions of the angels will be to gather the elect.

We have heretofore noted that as part of the Restoration,

Moses, the prophet and law-giver of ancient Israel, the one cho-sen of God to lead his people out of Egyptian bondage, came to Joseph Smith and Oliver Cowdery and committed to them "the keys of the gathering of Israel from the four parts of the earth, and the leading of the ten tribes from the land of the north" (D&C 110:11). Those keys are now vested in the president of The Church of Jesus Christ of Latter-day Saints.

After the Lord Jesus had set up his kingdom in the meridian of time; after he had spent forty days with his disciples as a resur-rected personage, teaching them all "things pertaining to the kingdom of God" that they should know at that time; and when he was ready to ascend to his Father, the disciples asked him, "Lord, wilt thou at this time restore again the kingdom to Israel?" They already had his church, but they were looking forward to the day when Israel as a people and as a nation would be gathered together and given again a high status among the nations of the earth (see Acts 1:3–6).

Jesus answered that this glorious eventuality was not for their day, that they were to do their assigned labors, and it was not for them "to know the times or the seasons, which the Father hath put in his own power" (Acts 1:7). Then he ascended into heaven, leaving to a future and distant day the establishment of the king-dom among the lost and scattered sheep of Israel—leaving the fulfillment of that divine promise to a day when the gospel would be restored by angelic ministrations—leaving it to a day when the decree would go forth that the restored gospel should be preached "to every nation, and kindred, and tongue, and people" (Revelation 14:6).

That time is now. With the authoritive "Listen to the voice of Jesus Christ, your Redeemer, the Great I AM," Joseph Smith and six other elders were told in September 1830, "Verily, I say unto you that ye are chosen out of the world to declare my gospel with the sound of rejoicing, as with the voice of a trump. . . . And ye are called to bring to pass the gathering of mine elect; for mine elect hear my voice" (D&C 29:1, 4, 7). Bear in mind that one proper use of the term angels is to denote righteous mortal men on the Lord's errand. Those who are properly "chosen out of the world to declare my gospel" and "bring to pass the gathering of mine elect" are angels.

The gathering of the elect is a great missionary undertaking. It is a matter of inviting scattered Israel to return to the Lord their God; to worship once again the God of Abraham and of Isaac and of Jacob; to come unto the Lord and forsake their false creeds. It is a call to worship that God who made them. These are "the servants of God" going forth and "saying with a loud voice: Fear God and give glory to him, for the hour of his judgment is come; And worship him that made heaven, and earth, and the sea, and the fountains of waters" (D&C 133:38–39).

TO MINISTER TO MEN

One of the most usual and, comfortingly, primary functions of angels is to minister to men in the flesh. To the psalmist it was given to understand this: "For he shall give his angels charge over thee, to keep thee in all thy ways. They shall bear thee up in their hands" (Psalm 91:11–12). The apostle Paul was given to understand this and spoke plainly about ministering spirits: "And of the angels he saith, Angels are ministering spirits" (Inspired Version, Hebrews 1:7; see also Hebrews 1:14).

To the devout, God-fearing centurion, Cornelius, God sent an angel who said, "Thy prayers and thine alms are come up for a memorial before God" (Acts 10:4). Having thus comforted Cornelius, the angel sent him to Peter, who could both tell him what was necessary for him to do to be saved and authoritatively administer the ordinances necessary (see Acts 10:1–10). From this experience we discern a secondary lesson. The angel did not administer the ordinances of salvation when there was an authorized mortal who could do it. He sent Cornelius to Peter, who could tell him what he "oughtest to do."

Of Nephi who was ministering during Christ's visitation on the American continent it is written, "So great was his faith on the Lord Jesus Christ that angels did minister unto him daily" (3 Nephi 7:18). This should serve as a prototype for us. Such was not an altogether unusual occurrence among the faithful. Many "saw the heavens open; and angels came down out of heaven and ministered unto them" (Helaman 5:48). "And angels did appear unto men, wise men, and did declare unto them glad tidings of great joy" (Helaman 16:14).

> And as they looked to behold they cast their eyes towards heaven, and they saw the heavens open, and they saw angels descending out of heaven as it were in the midst of fire; and they came down and encircled those little ones about, and they were encircled about with fire; and the angels did minister unto them. (3 Nephi 17:24.)

The beloved John was promised by the Lord that he could have the righteous desire of his heart and "tarry till I come" (John 21:22). Modern revelation enhances our knowledge of this most interesting incident in our Lord's ministry and says of John: "I will make him as flaming fire and a ministering angel; he shall minister for those who shall be heirs of salvation who dwell on the earth" (D&C 7:6).

When the priesthood of Aaron was restored to the earth, in our day, we were told that it "holds the keys of the ministering of angels" (D&C 13). Clearly this function of the angels is and ought to be enjoyed by the Saints.

TO MINISTER TO DISEMBODIED SPIRITS

Jurisdiction of the angels is not confined to men in the flesh. Quite obviously the acquiring of evidence of their activities out of our sphere is difficult. However, Luke records the words of Jesus relative to a certain rich man and Lazarus and what happened to them after their earthly deaths. The telling sheds light on a function of angels not otherwise catalogued. The Lord is quoted as saying that when one of the men died, his spirit was taken by the angels to the bosom of Abraham. It appears then that one function of angels is to assist in God's purposes after man's earthly probation. The pertinent verses read: "And it came to pass, that the beggar died, and was carried by the angels into Abraham's bosom:

the rich man also died, and was buried; And in hell he lift up his eyes . . ." (Luke 16:22–23). From this we may conclude that angels work with disembodied spirits.

This is in harmony with the scriptural concept that there are no dead unto God; all are alive unto him. The living and the dead are simply in various stages of progression. There is no such thing as death as far as God is concerned (see Matthew 22:32). God's purposes continue after this life.

TO MINISTER TO RESURRECTED PERSONAGES

As angelic functions continue into the spirit world, so they continue after the resurrection and judgment. Those who are assigned to the terrestrial glory will be ministered to by persons of the celestial glory. "And also the telestial receive it of the administering of angels who are appointed to minister for them, or who are appointed to be ministering spirits for them" (D&C 76:88).

> For these angels did not abide my law; therefore, they cannot be enlarged, but remain separately and singly, without exaltation, in their saved condition, to all eternity; and from henceforth are not gods, but are angels of God forever and ever. (D&C 132:17.)

These, "when they are out of the world . . . are appointed angels in heaven, which angels are ministering servants, to minister for those who are worthy of a far more, and an exceeding, and an eternal weight of glory" (D&C 132:16). These angels are in a saved condition. That is, they are saved from death and hell and are resurrected with bodies of celestial glory. However, they do not have the fulness of those "who keep their second estate" and thus "have glory added upon their heads for ever and ever" (Abraham 3:26). They minister to their brethren who have received "my Father's kingdom; therefore all that my Father hath shall be given unto [them]" (D&C 84:38). Although angels are directed to do God's purposes, there is a difference between being an angel and a god. Of those who have all that the Father has, it is said: "Then shall they be gods, because they have all power, and the angels are subject unto them." Such beings have "exaltation and continuation of the lives" (D&C 132:20, 22). Those who continue as angels do not (see D&C 132:16).

TO WORSHIP GOD

Worship consists of paying divine honors to a deity. The Father and the Son are the objects of all true worship. "All men should honour the Son, even as they honour the Father. He that honoureth not the Son honoureth not the Father which hath sent him" (John 5:23). "Thou shalt worship the Lord thy God, and him only shalt thou serve" (Matthew 4:10; see also Exodus 34:14; Mosiah 18:25; D&C 20:17–19). These divine fiats apply equally to men and to angels.

In point of fact, the Lord specifically requires worship by his angels. "And again, when he bringeth in the firstbegotten into the world, he saith, And let all the angels of God worship him" (Hebrews 1:6).

Angels are included in the requirement: "Praise ye the Lord. Praise ye the Lord from the heavens: praise him in the heights. Praise ye him, all his angels: praise ye him, all his hosts" (Psalm 148:1–2).

One of the proper functions of angels, as with the rest of us, is to worship God. When John was given a vision of the future heavens, he saw and "heard the voice of many angels round about the throne . . . Saying with a loud voice, Worthy is the Lamb . . . And every creature which is in heaven, and on the earth, and under the earth, and such as are in the sea, and all that are in them, heard I saying, Blessing, and honour, and glory, and power, be unto him that sitteth upon the throne, and unto the Lamb for ever and ever" (Revelation 5:11–13).

TO PROTECT MEN

There are many instances in which angels have saved men from perilous circumstances. Faithful people have repeatedly been guarded and watched over. Whole groups have been preserved, such as when the angel of the Lord's presence saved Israel (see Isaiah 7–9; D&C 133:53).

The Lord whispered to David, "The angel of the Lord encampeth round about them that fear him, and delivereth them" (Psalm 34:7). In the psalm of Moses, it is said, "There shall no evil befall thee, neither shall any plague come nigh thy dwelling. For he shall give his angels charge over thee, to keep thee in all thy ways. They shall bear thee up in their hands, lest thou dash thy foot against a stone" (Psalm 91:10–11).

Perhaps the best-known instance of an angel being dispatched by God to guard a righteous man is the case of Daniel. Daniel had been cast into a den of lions. The king fasted and prayed throughout the night for Daniel and in the morning said, "O Daniel, servant of the living God, is thy God, whom thou servest continually, able to deliver thee from the lions?" Daniel replied, "My God hath sent his angel, and hath shut the lions' mouths, that they have not hurt me" (Daniel 6:20–22).

On a similar mission an angel stopped Nephi's brothers from beating him (see 1 Nephi 3:29–31). In truth, the Lord does "encamp about" the righteous (see Zechariah 9:8). One of the functions of angels is to protect and guard us.

This well-known function of angels has given rise to a false assumption on the part of some scripture-reading people. The unwarranted assumption is that all men—or if not that, at least those who are righteous—have guardian angels. The fact that angels have intervened to preserve someone in a particular perilous circumstance does not establish the fact that people generally have guardian angels, any more than the fact that angels have otherwise ministered to selected persons would prove that angels have so ministered to men generally.

Every person born into the world is accorded protecting care by God. Such preserving care is provided by the Light of Christ (see D&C 84:44–118; Moroni 7:12–19). God-fearing people are often guarded against evil in compliance with its promptings. In addition to the Light of Christ, baptized persons have the gift of the Holy Ghost. By virtue of this endowment we may receive enlightenment and thereby be guarded and shielded (see D&C 8:2–4).

There is no scriptural justification for the tradition that a particular angel is assigned to one throughout one's life as a guardian angel. Such a procedure would appear to run counter to the known manner in which a benevolent Lord watches over his mortal children. The term guardian angel is a figure of speech that usually has reference to God's protecting care or an angel dispatched in God's purposes such as was the case with Daniel.

TO REAP

Angels are now reaping the earth. On the second day of January 1831, the Lord announced: "The angels are waiting the great command to reap down the earth, to gather the tares that they may be burned; and, behold, the enemy is combined" (D&C 38:12; see also D&C 86:5). All of this is in accordance with the teachings given by Jesus during his earthly ministry. Interpreting the parable of the tares, the Lord said:

> He that soweth the good seed is the Son of man;
> The field is the world; the good seed are the children of the kingdom; but the tares are the children of the wicked one;
> The enemy that sowed them is the devil; the harvest is the end of the world; and the reapers are the angels.
> As therefore the tares are gathered and burned in the fire; so shall it be in the end of this world.
> The Son of man shall send forth his angels, and they shall gather out of his kingdom all things that offend, and them which do iniquity:
> And shall cast them into a furnace of fire: there shall be wailing and gnashing of teeth. (Matthew 13:37–42.)

One of the presidents of the Church has told us that this day has come. "God has held the angels of destruction for many years, lest they should reap down the wheat with the tares. But I want to tell you now, that those angels have left the portals of heaven, and they stand over this people and this nation now, and are hovering over the earth waiting to pour out the judgments. And from this very day they shall be poured out. Calamities and troubles are increasing in the earth, and there is a meaning to these things" (*Discourses of Wilford Woodruff,* 230).

One of the functions of the angels is to be reapers.

TO DESTROY

Closely akin to reaping is the function of destroying. To some angels is given power to hurt the earth: "And I saw another angel ascending from the east, having the seal of the living God: and he cried with a loud voice to the four angels, to whom it was given to hurt the earth" (Revelation 7:2).

One means of preparing men for the truth is to humble them through affliction. Human nature has not changed much since the confrontation between Moses and Pharaoh when the Lord said, "How long wilt thou refuse to humble thyself before me? let my people go, that they may serve me" (Exodus 10:3). The terrible consequences of this confrontation are chronicled in the book of Exodus (see Exodus 7–12).

Since that awful time millions of people annually practice the rite of the Passover. "For I will pass through the land of Egypt this night, and will smite all the firstborn . . . I will execute judgment: I am the Lord" (Exodus 12:12). The one with power to save has power to destroy. "There is one lawgiver, who is able to save and to destroy" (James 4:12). The scriptures have since referred to this incident as a time the destroying angel passed by the children of Israel, and in our day, contingent upon our keeping God's commandments, we are told: "And I, the Lord, give unto them a promise, that the destroying angel shall pass by them, as the children of Israel, and not slay them" (D&C 89:21).

Luke, in the Acts of the Apostles, records an incident of a destroying angel. "And immediately the angel of the Lord smote him, because he gave not God the glory: and he was eaten of worms, and gave up the ghost" (Acts 12:23).

Some of the errands to which some angels will be and have been assigned are missions of destruction.

ALL NEEDFUL WORKS IN GOD'S PURPOSES

So diverse are the assignments of the angels that it does not serve a useful purpose here to further categorize the purposes and functions incident to angelic administrators. Suffice it to say that all needful works relative to God's purposes may be delegated to his created children, the angels. Some of their recorded activities that would not logically fall into the categories aforementioned would be:

1. Assists one of the women Jesus loved

> In the end of the sabbath, as it began to dawn toward the first day of the week, came Mary Magdalene and the other Mary to see the sepulchre.
>
> And, behold, there was a great earthquake: for the angel of the Lord descended from heaven, and came and rolled back the stone from the door, and sat upon it.
>
> His countenance was like lightning, and his raiment white as snow:
>
> And for fear of him the keepers did shake, and became as dead men.
>
> And the angel answered and said unto the women, Fear not ye: for I know that ye seek Jesus, which was crucified.
>
> He is not here: for he is risen, as he said. Come, see the place where the Lord lay.
>
> And go quickly, and tell his disciples that he is risen from the dead; and, behold, he goeth before you into Galilee; there shall ye see him: lo, I have told you. (Matthew 28:1–7.)

2. Opens prison doors

> But the angel of the Lord by night opened the prison doors, and brought them forth, and said,
>
> Go, stand and speak in the temple to the people all the words of this life. (Acts 5:19–20.)

3. Unlooses bands

> And as they lifted up their hands upon me, that they might offer me up and take away my life, behold, I lifted up my voice unto the Lord my God, and the Lord hearkened and heard, and he filled me with the vision of the Almighty, and

the angel of his presence stood by me, and immediately unloosed my bands. (Abraham 1:15.)

4. Detects the devil

The voice of Michael . . . detecting the devil when he appeared as an angel of light! (D&C 128:20.)

It seems to me that this is a sufficient listing to indicate a general pattern of using angels as a medium between God and man. We shall hereafter consider the truthfulness of Mormon's teachings, that "neither have angels ceased to minister unto the children of men" (Moroni 7:29).

MINISTRATIONS AFTER RESURRECTION COMPLETED

After the resurrection is completed, when the spirits and bodies of all personages connected with earth have been inseparably connected, there will still be ministration of angels. Certain resurrected personages will have assignments to minister to other resurrected personages who were their former fellow mortals. For instance, resurrected persons in the terrestrial kingdom will serve as ministering spirits to other resurrected persons in the telestial kingdom (D&C 76:88; Hebrews 1:14). Certain resurrected persons in the celestial kingdom will serve as "ministering servants" to other resurrected persons in a more exalted sphere of the celestial kingdom (see D&C 132:16–17).

The ministration of angels is an eternal reality.

*There is
rank and
precedence
among the
angels*

ORDER OF ANGELS

Very little has been revealed about the organization that exists among angelic beings. However, both modern and ancient scriptures indicate that an organization does exist. Some of the angels are designated by name. Some are not. The New Testament and the Doctrine and Covenants tell us by name who is the chief one of the angels (see 1 Thessalonians 4:16; Jude 9; D&C 29:26; 88:112; 107:54; 128:21). This is designation by rank. We thus know that there is a celestial hierarchy.

John the Revelator declares that some angels are stronger than others and that some angels are greater than others. He records, "And I saw a strong angel . . ." (Revelation 5:2). The implication of this terminology is clear. There are differing orders of angels. Angels have various assignments and various capabilities to accomplish the assigned tasks. Some of the tasks are more significant than others and require more power and authority in their performance. Some angels are granted more power and have more authority than others.

A modern Apostle puts it simply: "As with men, so with angels. Some are greater than others. There is rank and precedence, and there are varying degrees of power and might among God's ministers" (Bruce R. McConkie, *Doctrinal New Testament Commentary*, 3:471).

Although holy writ does not detail the complex structure, complete with lines of authority that would seem to exist, we are given much useful knowledge about some angels, their place in the system of things, and their job descriptions. We will now distill this knowledge from the scriptures.

MICHAEL

Michael is designated as an archangel. An archangel is a chief angel. Michael is the only angel so designated in the scriptures. This appellation is repeatedly used both in modern scripture and in the New Testament. In terms of rank he is thus the most prominent of all angels. He is the ranking angel. There is no angel of higher status. He is the first angel in the celestial hierarchy.

In our pre-earth life, "Michael was the most intelligent, powerful, and mighty spirit son of God, who was designated to come to this earth, excepting only the Firstborn, under whose direction and pursuant to whose counsel he worked" (McConkie, *Mormon Doctrine*, 491).

Michael's part in the creation of this earth was second only to that of Christ (Ibid.; see also Abraham 3:22–24).

When Satan rebelled against the Father in our pre-earth life, and there was war in heaven, it was Michael who led the hosts of the faithful in casting Satan out (see Revelation 12:7–9). I, for one, praise his name for my association with him there.

When the time came for the earth to be peopled, the spirit Michael was assigned to become the first mortal man, and he became known as Adam. He is thus referred to in the book of Daniel as the Ancient of Days. We are indebted to the inspiration of the Prophet Joseph for this invaluable information about Michael, Adam, the Ancient of Days: "Daniel in his seventh chapter speaks of the Ancient of Days; he means the oldest man, our Father Adam, Michael. . . ." (*TPJS*, 157.) As the first man, he fulfilled his foreordained destiny as the first (under Christ) in priesthood hierarchy. The Prophet Joseph continued, "He (Adam) is the father of the human family, and *presides over the spirits of all men*" (ibid.; italics added). "It is through him that Christ is revealed, that all revelation comes, that the Lord's affairs on earth are directed during the pre-millennial era" (McConkie, *Mormon Doctrine*, 491; see also *TPJS*, 157–59, 167–69).

Three years before he died, Adam called together his family in the valley of Adam-ondi-Ahman. "And the Lord appeared unto them, and they rose up and blessed Adam, and called him Michael, the prince, the archangel" (D&C 107:54). Michael was given "the keys of salvation under the counsel and direction of the Holy One" (D&C 78:16). That is, he holds the keys of salvation for all men associated with this earth, under Jesus only.

The angel Michael has been much in evidence over his stewardship. He contended with the devil over the body of Moses (see Jude 9). He ministered comfort to the prophet Daniel (see Daniel 10:13, 21). He appeared to Joseph Smith to detect "the devil when he appeared as an angel of light" (see D&C 128:20). He appeared to Joseph Smith to confer keys and authorities (see D&C 128:21). He was with Christ in the resurrection (see D&C 133:54–55; Matthew 27:52–53).

Michael will yet play an important role in the matters of this earth. He will convene another council at Adam-ondi-Ahman just prior to the dreadful day of the Lord. At that time all persons who have served under his direction will give an accounting of their ministry and stewardships. Jesus Christ will come and receive from father Adam (Michael) and all others a final accounting (see D&C 116; Daniel 7:9–14, 21–22, 26–27). Michael will partake of the sacrament with Christ and others (see D&C 27:11). He shall fight the battle of the Saints "at the time of the end" (see Daniel 11:40; 12:1). He shall sound his trump and the dead shall come forth from their graves.

> But, behold, verily I say unto you, before the earth shall pass away, Michael, mine archangel, shall sound his trump, and then shall all the dead awake, for their graves shall be opened, and they shall come forth—yea, even all. (D&C 29:26.)

He will lead the armies of heaven against the hosts of hell in the final great battle when Lucifer is cast out eternally.

And so on, until the seventh angel shall sound his trump; and he shall stand forth upon the land and upon the sea, and swear in the name of him who sitteth upon the throne, that there shall be time no longer; and Satan shall be bound, that old serpent, who is called the devil, and shall not be loosed for the space of a thousand years.

And then he shall be loosed for a little season, that he may gather together his armies.

And Michael, the seventh angel, even the archangel, shall gather together his armies, even the hosts of heaven.

And the devil shall gather together his armies; even the hosts of hell, and shall come up to battle against Michael and his armies.

And then cometh the battle of the great God; and the devil and his armies shall be cast away into their own place, that they shall not have power over the Saints any more at all.

For Michael shall fight their battles, and shall overcome him who seeketh the throne of him who sitteth upon the throne, even the Lamb.

This is the glory of God, and the sanctified; and they shall not any more see death. (D&C 88:110–16.)

Michael the archangel—Father Adam—was one of the most noble characters who ever lived. We have mentioned his angelic functions only. In the flesh he was baptized (Moses 6:64–66), married for eternity, for there was no death at that time (Moses 3:21–25), had the fulness of the gospel (Moses 5:57–59), and endured to the end in righteousness for 930 years. All that he did was "under the counsel and direction of the Holy One" (D&C 78:16). He will finally reign over his righteous posterity in the patriarchal order for all eternity. He will be an angel no longer, not even the chief angel. He will be a god (see Smith, *Doctrines of Salvation*, 1:90–106; D&C 132).

GABRIEL

Second in the priesthood hierarchy among the angels is Gabriel. The Prophet Joseph Smith says simply: "Gabriel . . . stands next in authority to Adam in the Priesthood" (*TPJS*, 157). That is, in rank and precedent, Gabriel stands next to Michael the archangel.

Incident to his preeminent position in priestly authority we know that Gabriel was among the spirit children of God shown to Abraham in a vision of pre-earth life, and described as one of "the noble and great ones" who "wast chosen before . . . [he] wast born," and of whom the Lord said, "I will make my rulers" (Abraham 3:22–23). He was given the Melchizedek Priesthood there (see Alma 13:3–7).

It is assumed that he was among those to whom God said, "We will go down, for there is space there, and we will take of these materials, and we will make an earth whereon these may dwell" (Abraham 3:24). Joseph Fielding Smith, one of the finest Latter-day Saint students of the scriptures, commented: "It is true that Adam helped form the earth. He labored with our Savior Jesus Christ. I have a strong view or conviction that there were others who assisted them. Perhaps Noah . . . and those who were appointed to be rulers before the earth was formed" (*Doctrines of Salvation*, 1:74–75). It is believed that Gabriel helped form the earth, although the scriptures do not name him by name in this work.

When Gabriel was assigned to come to this earth, as his probationary estate, and take upon himself a mortal tabernacle, he was called Noah. For this insight into the eternal scheme of things we are once again indebted to the Prophet Joseph Smith, who wrote, "Noah, . . . is Gabriel" (*TPJS*, 157).

While in the flesh, Noah "was called of God" to be a presiding "high priest" and was the father of all living in this day, and to him was given the "dominion." He held priesthood "keys first on earth, and then in heaven" (ibid.).

Gabriel (Noah) proved himself well while in the flesh. "But Noah found grace in the eyes of the Lord. These are the generations of Noah: Noah was a just man and perfect in his generations, and Noah walked with God" (Genesis 6:8–9). One could hardly have a better report on a more successful probationary estate. He had the fulness of the gospel (see Smith, *Doctrines of Salvation*,

1:160), meaning all that pertains to exaltation in the celestial kingdom, and endured to the end of his long life in righteousness.

To the Bible-reading world, Gabriel is the most prominent of all of the angels. This stems from his incomparable, well-known errands to Zacharias: "And the angel answering said unto him, I am Gabriel, that stand in the presence of God; and am sent to speak unto thee, and to shew thee these glad tidings" (Luke 1:19); and subsequently to Mary: "And in the sixth month the angel Gabriel was sent from God unto a city of Galilee, named Nazareth, to a virgin espoused to a man whose name was Joseph, of the house of David; and the virgin's name was Mary" (Luke 1:26–27). He thus became the precursor of John the Baptist and, finally, the harbinger of the ultimate good news, the advent of God in the flesh. Well might his fame spread abroad!

Long before this especial business was entrusted to him, we have biblical evidence that Gabriel was a ministering angel to Daniel. He records: "Yea, whiles I was speaking in prayer, even the man Gabriel, whom I had seen in the vision . . . touched me" (Daniel 9:21). Gabriel had been called upon to help Daniel once before (see Daniel 8:16).

During his earth life Gabriel (Noah) "received a dispensation of warning when the whole world had fallen into apostasy" (see Smith, *Doctrines of Salvation*, 1:161). Noah was the head of a gospel dispensation. To fulfill his position in the restoration of all things Gabriel came in modern times and conferred the keys of his dispensation upon Joseph Smith: " . . . the voice of Gabriel . . . declaring . . . [his] dispensation, . . . rights, . . . keys, . . . honors, . . . majesty and glory, and the power of . . . priesthood. . . ." (D&C 128:21).

Probably because of his prominence in announcing the birth of our Lord, there is a sectarian tradition that Gabriel will blow his horn to herald the Resurrection. There is no scriptural justification for this tradition. In point of fact, as we have heretofore seen, it will be Michael the archangel who shall sound the trump at that great day (see D&C 88:106–116).

The position of Gabriel is secure. His inheritance will be with those who are perfect and walk with God.

RAPHAEL

The Bible contains no reference to the angel Raphael. The Prophet Joseph Smith did not record his rank or precedence among celestial beings. However, it is clear that this angel had a mortal existence and held keys of priesthood power during his earthly ministry. All this is made known to us because Raphael appeared to the Prophet Joseph Smith in modern times and conferred the keys of his dispensation. He was thus a principal participant in the great restoration of all things. His part is recorded in modern scripture.

> And again, the voice of God in the chamber of old Father Whitmer, in Fayette, Seneca county, and at sundry times, and in divers places . . . the voice . . . of Raphael, and of divers angels, from Michael or Adam down to the present time, all declaring their dispensation, their rights, their keys, their honors, their majesty and glory, and the power of their priesthood; giving line upon line, precept upon precept; here a little, and there a little; giving us consolation by holding forth that which is to come, confirming our hope! (D&C 128:21.)

In the foregoing citation it is said of Raphael that he declared his dispensation. This is in accord with the pattern set in the restoration of the dispensation of the fulness of times. All former and prior dispensations are to be gathered into one. All keys and powers of former dispensations are gathered into this last great, culminating dispensation (see Ephesians 1:10; D&C 27:13). Careful perusal of the scriptures indicates, in almost each instance, the name and personage of the angelic visitant who restored the keys of the basic biblical dispensations (see D&C 110). I say, *almost* all, because a ministrant from one of the major biblical dispensations is not listed by name or dispensation.

Because the Doctrine and Covenants states that Raphael declared his dispensation, and because the declaring of one biblical dispensation is not otherwise recorded in holy writ, I venture to speculate that Raphael is a ministrant from a missing dispensation—the dispensation of Enoch. A modern author joins me in this educated guess:

> As to Raphael's mortal identity, we can only speculate. We do know the personages, however, who restored the keys exercised in the various great dispensations mentioned in the Bible, with the exception of the dispensation of Enoch. An inference thus arises that Raphael may be Enoch or some other great prophet from his dispensation. (McConkie, *Mormon Doctrine*, 168.)

If Raphael were Enoch, he enjoyed a most remarkable mortal ministry. "And it came to pass that Enoch journeyed in the land, among the people; and as he journeyed, the Spirit of God descended out of heaven, and abode upon him" (Moses 6:26).

> And so great was the faith of Enoch that he led the people of God, . . . and he spake the word of the Lord, and the earth trembled, and the mountains fled, even according to his command; and the rivers of water were turned out of their course . . .
> And the Lord called his people ZION. . . .
> And Enoch and all his people walked with God, and he dwelt in the midst of Zion; and it came to pass that Zion was not, for God received it up into his own bosom; and from thence went forth the saying, ZION IS FLED. (Moses 7:13, 18, 69.)

Since then many persons "were caught up by the powers of heaven into Zion" (Moses 7:27). Zion has become the term to denote the pure in heart (see D&C 97:21). The apostle Paul uses the term "mount Sion" to refer to the abode of exalted beings, and says there are "an innumerable company of angels" there (Hebrews 12:22). The city of Enoch is the standard when translation is discussed. Would Raphael's keys include the power whereby men may be translated?

John the Revelator wrote: "And I saw seven angels which stood before God" (Revelation 8:2). Canonized scriptures do not further identify these angels. The apocryphal writings do purport to identify one of them. The apocryphal book of Tobit contains this statement: "I am Raphael, one of the seven holy angels, . . . which go in and out before the glory of the Holy One" (Tobit 12:15). I pass no judgment as to the correctness or validity of the cited apocryphal work. However, it is of note that modern scripture corroborates the name and existence of the prominent angel, Raphael.

MOSES

The resurrected Moses was one of the prominent angelic ministrants to the Prophet Joseph Smith, "that in the dispensation of the fulness of times he might gather together in one all things in Christ, both which are in heaven, and which are on earth" (Ephesians 1:10). That this verse from Paul's Epistle to the Ephesians applies to the Prophet was confirmed by the Lord himself. In a revelation to Joseph Smith in 1830, the Lord said:

> I have committed the keys of my kingdom, and a dispensation of the gospel for the last times; and for the fulness of times, in the which I will gather together in one all things, both which are in heaven, and which are on earth. (D&C 27:13.)

And how could all former dispensations be gathered into one grand dispensation of the fulness of times without the incomparable Moses? Certainly Moses has to be numbered among God's spirit children who are "the noble and great ones" (Abraham 3:22).

Surely Moses was one of those who in their premortal existence was numbered among those of whom God said, "These I will make my rulers" (Abraham 3:23). And it is certain that Moses was one of those invited to participate when the Lord declared, "We will go down, for there is space there, and we will take of these materials, and we will make an earth" (Abraham 3:24).

As with other prominent angels, Moses spent a mortal probation here. He was the mediator of the old covenant, even as

Jesus Christ was of the new (see Acts 3:22–24). It was said to Moses, "thou art in the similitude of mine only Begotten" (Moses 1:6). In prophetic power, spiritual insight, and leadership qualifications, Moses hardly has a peer. Indeed, his life and ministry is a prototype of the mortal life and ministry of our Lord himself.

As a translated angel, the lawgiver appeared to Peter, James, and John on the Mount of Transfiguration.

> And after six days Jesus taketh Peter, James, and John his brother, and bringeth them up into an high mountain apart,
>
> And was transfigured before them: and his face did shine as the sun, and his raiment was white as the light.
>
> And, behold, there appeared unto them Moses and Elias talking with him.
>
> Then answered Peter, and said unto Jesus, Lord, it is good for us to be here: if thou wilt, let us make here three tabernacles; one for thee, and one for Moses, and one for Elias. (Matthew 17:1–4.)

On that occasion Moses gave keys and authority to Peter, James, and John (see Alma 45:18–19; *TPJS*, 158; Smith, *Doctrines of Salvation*, 2:109–112).

Moses was changed from a translated being to a resurrected personage (see D&C 133:54–56).

As a resurrected angel, he ministered to men in the flesh and thus carried out his part in the great restitution of all things (see Acts 3:19). On the 3rd day of April, 1836, he appeared to Joseph Smith and Oliver Cowdery in the Kirtland Temple and committed to them the keys of the gathering of Israel and the leading of the ten tribes from the land of the north.

> After this vision closed, the heavens were again opened unto us; and Moses appeared before us, and committed unto us the keys of the gathering of Israel from the four parts of the earth, and the leading of the ten tribes from the land of the north. (D&C 110:11.)

These were the special powers and endowments that rested

with Moses in the kingdom during his mortal life. Moses was the leader of a dispensation (D&C 84:17–28).

By virtue of the restoration of these keys, men are now authorized to use the priesthood for the gathering of Israel and the leading of the ten tribes. The time has finally arrived that Jesus' apostles asked him about when they said, "Lord, wilt thou at this time restore again the kingdom to Israel?" (Acts 1:6).

Now all things can be gathered together in Christ.

PETER, JAMES, AND JOHN

Peter, James, and John constituted the First Presidency of the Church of Jesus Christ as it existed in their day. To a counselor in the First Presidency among the Latter-day Saints, the Lord said: "I have given [to Joseph Smith] the keys of the kingdom, which belong always unto the Presidency of the High Priesthood" (D&C 81:2). Though there is no New Testament account of the organization of the First Presidency as a separate quorum among the former-day Saints, apparently these three, as the leading Apostles, functioned in this position while serving also in the Quorum of the Twelve Apostles.

The New Testament is explicit and detailed in rendering the account of our Lord himself giving the keys of the kingdom to Peter.

> When Jesus came into the coasts of Caesarea Philippi, he asked his disciples, saying, Whom do men say that I the Son of man am?
>
> And they said, Some say that thou art John the Baptist: some, Elias; and others, Jeremias, or one of the prophets.
>
> He saith unto them, But whom say ye that I am?
>
> And Simon Peter answered and said, Thou are the Christ, the Son of the living God.
>
> And Jesus answered and said unto him, Blessed art thou, Simon Bar-jona: for flesh and blood hath not revealed it unto thee, but my Father which is in heaven.
>
> And I say also unto thee, That thou art Peter, and upon this rock I will build my church; and the gates of hell shall not prevail against it.

> And I will give unto thee the keys of the kingdom of heaven: and whatsoever thou shalt bind on earth shall be bound in heaven: and whatsoever thou shalt loose on earth shall be loosed in heaven. (Matthew 16:13–19.)

Even Christ had been called to the Holy Priesthood. "Thou art a priest for ever after the order of Melchisedec," Paul explains of Jesus (Hebrews 7:17). In this, as in all things, Christ was our perfect example and prototype (see *TPJS*, 318). He told us that men could neither choose nor ordain themselves. Man does not take this "heavenly calling" (Hebrews 3:1) upon himself; he must be "called of God" to be "an high priest after the order of Melchisedec" (Hebrews 5:10). "Ye have not chosen me, but I have chosen you, and ordained you," Jesus told those he had called to the holy priesthood (John 15:16). Peter wrote of the "holy" and "royal priesthood" with which he had been empowered (1 Peter 2:5, 9).

In June 1829, on the banks of the Susquehanna River, Peter, James, and John appeared to Joseph Smith and Oliver Cowdery. They were functioning as angelic ministrants. Peter and James were resurrected persons; John was a translated personage (see John 21:20–23). This was a necessary part of the bringing together of all things in the dispensation of the fulness of times. The scriptural record of their visitation reads:

> And also with Peter, and James, and John, whom I have sent unto you, by whom I have ordained you and confirmed you to be apostles, and especial witnesses of my name, and bear the keys of your ministry and of the same things which I revealed unto them;
>
> Unto whom I have committed the keys of my kingdom, and a dispensation of the gospel for the last times; and for the fulness of times, in the which I will gather together in one all things, both which are in heaven, and which are on earth;
>
> And also with all those whom my Father hath given me out of the world. (D&C 27:12–14.)

In an epistle from Joseph Smith the Prophet to the Latter-day Saints in Nauvoo, Illinois, reference is again made to this wondrous occasion: "The voice of Peter, James, and John in the wilderness between Harmony, Susquehanna county, and Colesville, Broome county, on the Susquehanna river, declaring themselves as possessing the keys of the kingdom, and of the dispensation of the fulness of times!" (D&C 128:20).

These angels restored to the earth the following: the Melchizedek Priesthood; the keys of the kingdom of God, including the commission to preach the gospel in all the world; and the keys of the dispensation of the fulness of times.

Peter, James, and John had been ministered to by angels during their mortal ministry. Two angels, in this instance translated beings, appeared to them, in the presence of a transfigured Jesus, and with evidence of the presence of the Eternal Father, and gave keys to them. "The Savior, Moses, and Elias, gave the keys to Peter, James and John, on the mount, when they were transfigured before him" (*TPJS*, 158). The New Testament tells of this experience with angels as follows:

> And after six days Jesus taketh Peter, James, and John his brother, and bringeth them up into an high mountain apart,
> And was transfigured before them: and his face did shine as the sun, and his raiment was white as the light.
> And, behold, there appeared unto them Moses and Elias talking with him.
> Then answered Peter, and said unto Jesus, Lord, it is good for us to be here: if thou wilt, let us make here three tabernacles; one for thee, and one for Moses, and one for Elias.
> While he yet spake, behold, a bright cloud overshadowed them: and behold a voice out of the cloud, which said, This is my beloved Son, in whom I am well pleased; hear ye him. (Matthew 17:1–5.)

In their visitation to Joseph Smith and Oliver Cowdery, these angels were doing what they had seen done before. They passed on keys and powers and authorities that, in turn, had been given to them by Jesus and by other angelic ministrants. The course of God is one eternal round.

MORONI

John the Revelator was given a comprehensive vision that sheds forth a blaze of light. His is a voice that tells of the restoration of eternal truth. Other major prophets saw the same things but were under a restriction not to write them because they were to be written by John (see 1 Nephi 14:25–27). An important part of John's vision has to do with this discussion:

> And I saw another angel fly in the midst of heaven, having the everlasting gospel to preach unto them that dwell on the earth, and to every nation, and kindred, and tongue, and people,
> Saying with a loud voice, Fear God, and give glory to him; for the hour of his judgment is come: and worship him that made heaven, and earth, and the sea, and the fountains of waters. (Revelation 14:6–7.)

John saw the last days when the everlasting gospel would be revealed by angelic messengers.

The coming of Moroni was in partial fulfillment of John's vision of another angel flying in the midst of heaven to commit the everlasting gospel to man. On the third day of November, 1831, the Lord said to his Saints:

> And now, verily saith the Lord, that these things might be known among you, O inhabitants of the earth, I have sent forth mine angel flying through the midst of heaven, having the everlasting gospel, who hath appeared unto some and hath committed it unto man, who shall appear unto many that dwell on the earth.
> And this gospel shall be preached unto every nation, and kindred, and tongue, and people. (D&C 133:36–37.)

Moroni was the selected angel for this errand because he was the one "to whom I have committed the keys of the record of the stick of Ephraim" (D&C 27:5). The Lord uses the same termi-nology here as he did to Ezekiel when he referred to the history of some of the descendants of Joseph as "the stick of Ephraim" (Ezekiel 37:16). It was Moroni who was sent "to reveal the Book of Mormon, containing the fulness of my everlasting gospel" (D&C 27:5). Clearly, Moroni was the one to whom John referred.

We have heretofore quoted at length from Joseph Smith's account of the happening on 21 September 1823, when the Angel Moroni appeared to him and gave him instructions (see Joseph Smith–History 1:27–49). This is the most detailed writing in existence of an angelic visitation. In a subsequent revelation the Prophet Joseph Smith refers to that wondrous night. "And again, what do we hear? Glad tidings from Cumorah! Moroni, an angel from heaven, declaring the fulfillment of the prophets—the book to be revealed" (D&C 128:20).

As with other angelic ministrants, Moroni spent a probationary estate here. He lived on the American continent until about A.D. 421. He was the son of Mormon and helped his father in the task of making an abridgment of the records of their people (see Moroni 1:1; 7:1; Mormon 8:1). He was the final custodian in his day of the plates from which the Book of Mormon was to be translated (see Mormon 8). He prophesied that they would come "out of the earth" (Mormon 8:26) as had Isaiah before him (see Isaiah 29:4). Interestingly, in the final chapter in the Book of Mormon, Moroni exhorts us to "deny not the gifts of God" and lists as one of such gifts "the beholding of angels and ministering spirits" (Moroni 10:8, 14).

In reading his final exhortation one feels that he knew of his future angelic mission. He talks of his soon going "to rest in the paradise of God," but only until "my spirit and body shall again reunite, and I am brought forth triumphant through the air" (Moroni 10:34). Shades of "And I saw another angel fly in the midst of heaven"! (Revelation 14:6).

ELIJAH

For sheer drama and interest, the ministry of Elijah the prophet hardly has an equal. He sealed the heavens so that it did not rain; was fed by ravens; tested the widow woman almost beyond mortal strength, then extended her barrel of meal and cruse of oil, and then raised her son from death; destroyed the priests of Baal in one of history's most dramatic confrontations between good and evil; called down fire from heaven; fasted for forty days and forty nights; was ministered to by angels; heard and understood the "still small voice" of God; and was translated and taken into heaven without tasting death (see 1 Kings 17–19; 2 Kings 1–2). One might say he lived his life to the fullest.

He was also the subject of the last prophecy in the Old Testament:

> Behold, I will send you Elijah the prophet before the coming of the great and dreadful day of the Lord:
> And he shall turn the heart of the fathers to the children, and the heart of the children to their fathers, lest I come and smite the earth with a curse. (Malachi 4:5–6.)

He ministered in New Testament times as a translated being. As previously noted, Matthew writes of his angelic function:

> And after six days Jesus taketh Peter, James, and John his brother, and bringeth them up into an high mountain apart,
> And was transfigured before them: and his face did shine as the sun, and his raiment was white as the light.
> And behold, there appeared unto them Moses and Elias talking with him.
> Then answered Peter, and said unto Jesus, Lord, it is good for us to be here: if thou wilt, let us make here three tabernacles; one for thee, and one for Moses, and one for Elias. (Matthew 17:1–4.)

The purpose and function of these angels in attending the called leaders of the Church on earth was to give them keys and powers. Quoting Joseph Smith, President Joseph Fielding Smith said: "The Savior, Moses, and Elias [Elijah, in other words], gave the keys to Peter, James and John, on the mount, when they were transfigured before him" (*TPJS*, 158). He goes on to suggest that Moses and Elijah were preserved from death by translation to perform this very mission, in the flesh, and prior to the resurrection.

The Angel Moroni told Joseph Smith that Elijah would be

sent to reveal to him certain priesthood powers (see Joseph Smith–History 1:38–39). Incident to the work in which he had heretofore participated, and in fulfillment of prophecy by Malachi and Moroni, Elijah did come to Joseph Smith and Oliver Cowdery in the Kirtland Temple on 3 April 1836. His coming is recorded in modern scripture.

> After this vision had closed, another great and glorious vision burst upon us; for Elijah the prophet, who was taken to heaven without tasting death, stood before us, and said:
>
> Behold, the time has fully come, which was spoken of by the mouth of Malachi—testifying that he [Elijah] should be sent, before the great and dreadful day of the Lord come—
>
> To turn the hearts of the fathers to the children, and the children to the fathers, lest the whole earth be smitten with a curse—
>
> Therefore, the keys of this dispensation are committed into your hands; and by this ye may know that the great and dreadful day of the Lord is near, even at the doors. (D&C 110:13–16.)

Elijah thus participated, as a major principal, in the bringing together into one all things in the dispensation of the fulness of times. His was such a fundamental contribution that Joseph Smith discoursed on it upon several occasions. Elijah gave the keys of full salvation for the living and the dead. He "was the last Prophet that held the keys of the Priesthood" in ancient Israel, the Prophet said. His latter-day mission was to "restore the authority and deliver the keys of the Priesthood, in order that all the ordinances may be attended to in righteousness. . . . Why send Elijah? Because he holds the keys of the authority to administer in all the ordinances of the Priesthood; and without the authority is given, the ordinances could not be administered in righteousness" (*TPJS*, 172).

> Now for Elijah. The spirit, power, and calling of Elijah is, that ye have power to hold the key of revelations, ordinances, oracles, powers and endowments of the fulness of the Melchizedek Priesthood and of the kingdom of God on the

earth; and to receive, obtain, and perform all the ordinances belonging to the kingdom of God, even unto the turning of the hearts of the fathers unto the children, and the hearts of the children unto the fathers, even those who are in heaven. . . .

What is this . . . work of Elijah? . . . [It is] to seal the children to the fathers, and the fathers to the children. . . .

. . . this is the spirit of Elijah, that we redeem our dead, and connect ourselves with our fathers which are in heaven . . . the power of Elijah [is] to seal those who dwell on earth to those who dwell in heaven. (Ibid., 337–38.)

In short, the coming of Elijah in this dispensation makes salvation available for the dead as well as the living. Such is the sealing power of Elijah!

ELIAS OF ABRAHAM'S DAY

Elias is both a name and a title. There are many Eliases. According to the plan and program of the Lord, the dispensation of the fulness of times is "the times of restitution of all things, which God hath spoken by the mouth of all his holy prophets since the world began" (Acts 3:21). This restoration is to be effected by Elias. The promise is: "Elias truly shall first come, and restore all things" (Matthew 17:11). We have already demonstrated that many angelic ministrants have been sent to confer keys and commit their dispensations to men on earth. We have examined the contributions to this end of Michael, Gabriel, Raphael, Moses, Peter, James, John, Moroni, and Elijah. No one messenger carried the whole burden of the restoration. Each has come with specific endowments. It seems clear that Elias is a composite personage. "The expression [Elias] must be understood to be a name and a title for those whose mission it was to commit keys and powers to men in this final dispensation" (McConkie, *Mormon Doctrine*, 221; see also Smith, *Doctrines of Salvation*, 1:170–74). Various scriptural citations to Elias properly refer to different persons (see Inspired Version, John 1:21–28; D&C 27:6–7; 77:9, 14).

The Elias of Abraham's day came to Joseph Smith and Oliver

Cowdery on 3 April 1836 in the Kirtland Temple and played a role in the restoration of all things. We have no information as to his mortal life or ministry. We do not know if his name was Elias in the flesh. We do not know whether it was Abraham himself. We do know that an angelic visitor, representing the dispensation of Abraham, came. "After this, Elias appeared, and committed the dispensation of the gospel of Abraham, saying that in us and our seed all generations after us should be blessed" (D&C 110:12).

What did this Elias give to the earth again? The gospel of Abraham. And what is the gospel of Abraham? What is that portion of the good news of salvation particularly associated with Abraham? It is a divine promise that his seed should continue "as innumerable as the stars; or, if ye were to count the sand upon the seashore ye could not number them" (D&C 132:30; see also Genesis 17; Abraham 2:1–12). This promise is to apply out of this world as well as in this world. The gospel especially associated with Abraham was the gospel of celestial marriage and the gospel of plural marriage. It is the commission to provide a lineage for the elect portion of the pre-earth spirits of the Eternal Father. It is a gospel to provide a mansion in heaven for those who lived the celestial law here. This is what was restored. As a result of this portion of the restoration, the righteous among future generations were assured of the continuation of seeds forever, even as it was with Abraham of old (see D&C 132).

JOHN THE BAPTIST

Gabriel foretold that John the Baptist would go before the Lord "in the spirit and power of Elias" (Luke 1:17). John was an Elias. When pressed by the unbelieving Jews, John said, "I am not that Elias who was to restore all things" (Inspired Version, John 1:22). His mission was to prepare the way before, to baptize, and to acclaim the divine Sonship of Christ (see John 1). These were singular honors. Thus, the Lord's statement: "Among those that are born of women there is not a greater prophet than John the Baptist" (Luke 7:28).

John was the last legal administrator, holding keys and authority under the Mosaic dispensation (see *TPJS*, 275–76). Within the Mosaic dispensation were the "key[s] of the ministering of angels and the preparatory gospel; which gospel is the gospel of repentance and of baptism, and the remission of sins" (D&C 84:26–27).

Because John was the last person on the earth to hold these powers and authorities, he was the uniquely qualified person to be sent to restore them as part of the dispensation of the fulness of times. As a resurrected being, he was dispatched to play his important role.

On the fifteenth day of May, 1829, he returned to the earth as an angel to confer the Aaronic Priesthood upon Joseph Smith and Oliver Cowdery (see Joseph Smith–History 1:68–70). He announced himself as John, the same that is called John the Baptist in the New Testament. The angelic visitant averred that he was acting under the direction of Peter, James, and John, the ancient apostles, who held the keys of the higher priesthood.

The prayer of ordination is recorded in the Doctrine and Covenants, section 13:

> Upon you my fellow servants, in the name of Messiah I confer the Priesthood of Aaron, which holds the keys of the ministering of angels, and of the gospel of repentance, and of baptism by immersion for the remission of sins; and this shall never be taken again from the earth, until the sons of Levi do offer again an offering unto the Lord in righteousness.

It is significant to note the promise that the priesthood thus restored would remain on the earth until "the sons of Levi . . . may offer unto the Lord an offering in righteousness"; that is, until Christ comes in his glory (see Malachi 3:3). So it is with all of the restoration of all things.

In a separate revelation, Joseph Smith was reminded that the Lord had sent John, who was "filled with the spirit of Elias; which John I have sent unto you . . . to ordain you unto the first priesthood which you have received, that you might be called and ordained even as Aaron" (D&C 27:7–8). Paul, in explaining the gospel to his Hebrew brethren, declares in similar terms, "And no man taketh this honour unto himself, but he that is called of God, as was Aaron" (Hebrews 5:4). The restoration of *all* things had to include the restoration of the Aaronic or lesser priesthood in the prophesied and scripturally prescribed manner.

This same angel, John, promised them there would yet be a fuller restoration and that in due time the priesthood of Melchizedek would also be conferred upon them (see *History of the Church* 1:39–41). We have heretofore seen that this prophecy was fulfilled to the letter.

Line upon line, precept upon precept, here a little and there a little, The Church of Jesus Christ of Latter-day Saints was wholly established upon the earth once again. And all of this by angelic visitations.

JOHN THE BELOVED

We have given account of the former-day First Presidency consisting of Peter, James, and John. In their historic role of restorers of the Melchizedek Priesthood and the keys of the kingdom and the keys of the dispensation of the fulness of times, they acted as a quorum.

Aside from this angelic role, one of them, John, ministers even now as an angel of God upon the earth. This remarkable New Testament incident is recorded by him to whom it happened.

> Then Peter, turning about, seeth the disciple whom Jesus loved following; which also leaned on his breast at supper, and said, Lord, which is he that betrayeth thee?
>
> Peter seeing him saith to Jesus, Lord, and what shall this man do?
>
> Jesus saith unto him, If I will that he tarry till I come, what is that to thee? follow thou me.
>
> Then went this saying abroad among the brethren, that that disciple should not die: yet Jesus said not unto him, He shall not die; but, If I will that he tarry till I come, what is that to thee?

This is the disciple which testifieth of these things, and wrote these things: and we know that his testimony is true. (John 21:20–24.)

"There be some standing here," Jesus said about the time Peter gave his famous testimony of our Lord's divine Sonship, "which shall not taste of death, till they see the Son of man coming in his kingdom" (Matthew 16:28). John is the only one of such of whom we have any knowledge. On that occasion Peter had just had a glimpse of his own future martyrdom and desired to know what awaited John. The answer was curious. He is to tarry in the flesh until Christ comes in his glory at the end of the world (see D&C 7:3, John 21:22–23).

Joseph Smith, as did other untold righteous men, wondered about this most unusual promise. He inquired of God as to whether John, the beloved disciple, tarried in the flesh or had died. He was given this answer:

> And the Lord said unto me: John, my beloved, what desirest thou? For if you shall ask what you will, it shall be granted unto you.
>
> And I said unto him: Lord, give unto me power over death, that I may live and bring souls unto thee.
>
> And the Lord said unto me: Verily, verily, I say unto thee, because thou desirest this thou shalt tarry until I come in my glory, and shalt prophesy before nations, kindreds, tongues and people.
>
> And for this cause the Lord said unto Peter: If I will that he tarry till I come, what is that to thee? For he desired of me that he might bring souls unto me, but thou desirest that thou mightest speedily come unto me in my kingdom.
>
> I say unto thee, Peter, this was a good desire; but my beloved has desired that he might do more, or a greater work yet among men than what he has before done.
>
> Yea, he has undertaken a greater work; therefore, I will make him as flaming fire and a ministering angel; he shall minister for those who shall be heirs of salvation who dwell on the earth.

And I will make thee to minister for him and for thy
brother James; and unto you three I will give this power and
the keys of this ministry until I come.

Verily I say unto you, ye shall both have according to
your desires, for ye both joy in that which ye have desired.
(D&C 7.)

John, a ministering angel, yet lives as a translated being, to
serve certain persons who shall be heirs of salvation.

THE THREE NEPHITES

Three of the Nephite disciples had the same desires in their
hearts as did John the Beloved during Jesus' earthly ministry.
They too received the righteous desires of their hearts as the risen
Lord said to them:

> Therefore, more blessed are ye, for ye shall never taste of
> death; but ye shall live to behold all the doings of the Father
> unto the children of men, even until all things shall be fulfilled
> according to the will of the Father, when I shall come in my
> glory with the powers of heaven. (3 Nephi 28:7.)

"And they are as the angels of God," the Book of Mormon
states (3 Nephi 28:30). Since the day of their "transfiguration,"
they "shall not have pain while [they] shall dwell in the flesh, neither sorrow save it be for the sins of the world. . . . They did
go forth upon the face of the land, and did minister unto all the
people . . . and did preach the gospel of Christ . . . among the
Gentiles . . . also . . . among the Jews." They were not known nor
recognized as translated beings (see 3 Nephi 28:9–28). Their ministry in the Americas continued for approximately three hundred
years, when they were finally withdrawn because of the wickedness of the people (see 4 Nephi; Mormon 1:13–16).

Unknown to the world they continue their ministry at this
very time. There are angels on the earth. Some people have, as
Paul says, "entertained angels unawares" (Hebrews 13:2).

These three disciples, as also presumably John, shall "never
taste of death"; but when Christ comes they "shall be changed in

73

the twinkling of an eye" and then shall "be blessed in the king-dom of my Father" (3 Nephi 28:7–8).

CHERUB, CHERUBIM

God's messengers, those individuals whom he sends to perform all things relative to his work, are called angels. Angels are chosen from among his offspring and are themselves in various stages of progression in their respective spheres.

Some such beings were assigned by God to guard the tree of life when Adam and Eve were cast out of the garden of Eden. "So he drove out the man; and he placed at the east of the garden of Eden Cherubims, and a flaming sword which turned every way, to keep the way of the tree of life" (Genesis 3:24; see also Moses 4:31). This kept them from partaking of the tree of life and pre-vented them from living forever in their sins.

This is a classical example of persons being assigned an errand in the purposes of God. In this instance the persons must have come from the presence of God, inasmuch as there were only two of his children then on the earth, Adam and Eve. Therefore, a cherub is an angel.

According to Webster's *New Collegiate Dictionary*, the plural for cherub is cherubs or cherubim. The foregoing Genesis citation from the King James Version of the Bible erroneously uses *cheru-bims* as the plural form. The footnoted Pearl of Great Price refer-ence uses the proper *cherubim*, as does the Book of Mormon (Alma 12:21; 42:2–3) and the Inspired Version of the Bible (Exodus 25:20–22). This is brought to the reader's attention to demonstrate that three separate works of scripture refer to angels known as cherubs or cherubim.

From the assignments so denoted in the scriptures, and from the fact that images of them were directed to be apart from the mercy seat of the ark in the Holy of Holies (see Exodus 25:18–20; 37:7–9), it appears that a cherub is an angel of some particular order or rank to whom specific duties and work are assigned. However, none of the standard works sets forth either the iden-tity or job description of these heavenly beings. Because Moses spoke with God in the Holy of Holies (Numbers 7:89), it is said that the images of cherubs there symbolize the presence of Jehovah in the midst of his people. "Give ear, O Shepherd of Israel, thou that leadest Joseph like a flock; thou that dwellest between the cherubims, shine forth" (Psalm 80:1).

Ezekiel had a vision in which he saw creatures: "And every one had four faces: the first face was the face of a cherub, and the second face . . . the face of a man, . . . third . . . a lion, . . . fourth . . . an eagle" (Ezekiel 10:14). He called them cherubims and said that each had "four wings" (Ezekiel 10:21). Thus, the images in Solomon's Temple are cherubs with wings (see 1 Kings 6:23–25). What Ezekiel saw was symbolical. His rendering of this vision is similar to John's vision wherein he saw beasts. The Prophet Joseph Smith was asked to interpret John's vision on beasts. "What are we to understand by . . . wings, which the beasts had? . . . Their wings are a representation of power, to move, to act, etc." (D&C 77:4). Such imagery is figurative. The same old Jewish imagery, or figure of speech, is used and its meaning made clear when it was said of the Lord, "And he rode upon a cherub, and did fly: and he was seen upon the wings of the wind" (2 Samuel 22:11). The same metaphorical use of "wings of the wind" is found in Psalms (see Psalm 18:10). As the wind has wings, so do cherubs have figurative wings.

The Prophet Joseph Smith put to rest the misapprehension abroad in the land that angels have wings when he authoritatively said, "An angel of God never has wings" (*TPJS*, 162).

SERAPH, SERAPHIM

Seraphim are angels who reside in the presence of God. It is clear that they include the unembodied spirits of our premortal existence, for our Lord "looked upon the wide expanse of eternity, and all the seraphic hosts of heaven, before the world was made" (D&C 38:1). Also, emerging out of Isaiah's colorful old Jewish idiom in describing his vision of seraphim, we find phraseology reminiscent of the great vision of premortal life: "Also I heard the voice of the Lord, saying, Whom shall I send, and who will go for us? . . . Here am I; send me" (Isaiah 6:8; see also Abraham 3:27).

One of the functions of the seraphim is to give honor, glory, and adoration to God. "Praise ye him, all his angels: praise ye him, all his hosts" (Psalm 148:2). While petitioning on behalf of the Saints, the Prophet Joseph Smith prayed that "we may mingle our voices with those bright, shining seraphs around thy throne, with acclamations of praise, singing Hosanna to God and the Lamb!" (D&C 109:79). To me this infers that the name *seraphs* may apply to angels other than premortal spirit children of the Eternal Father. Certainly there will be perfected and resurrected angels giving glory and adoration and worshiping God at his throne.

Isaiah saw the Lord in vision "sitting upon a throne, high and lifted up, and his train filled the temple. Above it stood the seraphims. . . . And one cried unto another, and said, Holy, holy, holy, is the Lord of hosts: the whole earth is full of his glory" (Isaiah 6:1–3). Once again, in old Judaic terminology, "each one had six wings; with twain he covered his face, and with twain he covered his feet, and with twain he did fly" (Isaiah 6:2). Apparently because of this vision, ancient Judaism looked upon seraphs as angels of the highest rank who were believed to guard God's throne with ardor.

The fact that these angels were shown to him as having six wings was to symbolize their power to move and to act. This is a situation that other major prophets have also visualized. John saw beasts for symbolic reasons. When asked for an explanation of the wings John saw on the beasts, Joseph Smith answered, "Their wings are a representation of power, to move, to act, etc." (D&C 77:4).

Seraphs are intelligent, moral beings before the throne of God. They are angels. The Prophet Joseph Smith tells us plainly, "An angel of God never has wings" (*TPJS*, 162). Seraphim do not have literal wings. They do declare the holiness of God and that "the whole earth is full of his glory" (Isaiah 6:3).

DIVERSE ANGELS

In grand, sweeping phrases the Prophet Joseph Smith writes an epistle to the Latter-day Saints, detailing the restoration of the fulness of times. He was such a superlative prophet. To him the veil was so thin. After naming the major angels we have heretofore considered, who had ministered to him, the Prophet recalled that he had heard the voice[s] of divers angels, . . . all declaring their . . . rights, their keys, their honors, their majesty and glory . . . ; giving line upon line, precept upon precept; here a little, and there a little" (D&C 128:21). The Prophet of the Restoration recorded what needed to be recorded. The world is not prepared to understand, let alone accept, the wealth of spiritual experiences that were his. But we are put on notice that there were less prominent angels than the ones listed by name and specific purposes. They also minister to men.

It is as though we are being told that words can't truly convey the majesty of what really happened. An outline is sketched for us—the mere skin of an idea. It says: Don't use strict construction in reading the visions of the prophets; ponder them in your heart; let the Spirit guide you.

And so men have speculated. The old Hebrew concept of the celestial hierarchy is said to consist of seven archangels. Two of these, Michael and Gabriel, are mentioned in the Bible and in the Doctrine and Covenants (see Jude 9; D&C 128:21). The name of a third, Raphael, is found in the Doctrine and Covenants (D&C 128:21) and the apocryphal book of Tobit (Tobit 3:17). The names of four others—Uriel, Raguel, Sariel, and Jerahmeel are found in a noncanonical, apocalyptic book, the Book of Enoch (Enoch 21). Apocryphal sources give the names of the last three as: Izidiel, Hanael, and Kepharel.

For the purposes of this writing we have thus far concerned ourselves only with scripturally documented discussions of angels. After all, from this accepted and credible source we have record of "many angels round about the throne . . . and the number of them was ten thousand times ten thousand, and thousands of thousands" (Revelation 5:11).

Knowledge of
good and evil
is the best fruit of
the tree of
knowledge

FALLEN ANGELS

The theory of good and evil is of fundamental importance in all moral life. It is the essence of ethics, economics, politics, jurisprudence, and rational and moral theology and religion. What concept is concerned more with human behavior? The basic terms of theology and religion—righteousness and sin, salvation and damnation—are, like virtue and vice, happiness and misery, conceptions of good and evil in the conditions of man. Those who give credence to holy writ consider the goodness or evil of man in terms of his relation to God.

God is good. Good is of God and consists in obedience to his laws and conformity to his mind and will. "Wherefore, all things which are good cometh of God . . . [and] that which is of God inviteth and enticeth to do good continually; wherefore, every thing which inviteth and enticeth to do good, and to love God, and to serve him, is inspired of God" (Moroni 7:12–13).

The scriptural concept of good consists in the knowledge of God: his personage, his attributes, his characteristics, and his perfections (see Joseph Smith, *Lectures on Faith*) and the putting on by man of His divine nature.

Philosophers and theologians historically have concerned themselves with what is traditionally called "the problem of evil." How are we to understand the existence of evil in a world created by a God who is omnipotent and perfectly good? To understand the nature and source of evil, together with its place in the eternal scheme of things, it is necessary to understand God's plan of salvation for all of his creatures, which is made known to us in the holy scriptures.

Evil is the opposite of good. It consists in disobeying the laws of God and contravening his will.

As far as men on this earth are concerned, evil had its beginning in a pre-earth existence. The Eternal Father begat children. That is, he clothed uncreated spirit element or intelligence with spirit bodies. We thus became conscious identities. There were eternal laws that existed for the good of said children. The children were endowed with agency, the ability to choose. Disobedience to those laws was in its nature evil. The possibility of committing evil was a necessary correlative to the possibility of keeping the laws. Lucifer and one-third of the spirits of heaven chose evil rather than good. They exercised their agency and did not act righteously. Finally, they came out in open rebellion against God. They were cast out onto the earth and were denied mortal bodies (see Moses 4:1–4; Abraham 3:24–28; D&C 29:36–40; Revelation 12:7–13). We will particularize, with appropriate annotations, each of these steps.

Having been cast out of the presence of God, Lucifer, the devil, and his followers, demons, continued their rebellion against God. It is their self-appointed mission to entice men to violate the laws of God and thereby commit evil. Thus, as far as this mortal life is concerned, Lucifer is the author and creator of evil, for evil is of the devil. "That which is evil cometh of the devil; for the devil is an enemy unto God, and fighteth against him continually, and inviteth and enticeth to sin, and to do that which is evil continually" (Moroni 7:12).

God does not tempt man to do evil. "Let no man say when he is tempted, I am tempted of God: for God cannot be tempted with evil, neither tempteth he any man" (James 1:13). Man has his agency. He has the ability to choose. "But every man is tempted, when he is drawn away of his own lust, and enticed" (James 1:14).

The presence of evil in this world is a reality without which the plan of salvation could not operate. "For it must needs be, that there is an opposition in all things" (2 Nephi 2:11). Without good as the opposite of bad, without righteousness as the opposite of evil, this world could not be the probationary estate to prove God's creatures in the flesh. The existence of evil—not the partaking of evil—is essential to the attainment of salvation.

The concept of good is inextricably connected to the God of the scriptures. So also, the concept of evil is a tangle from which it is impossible to unravel the devil of the scriptures. The biblical concept of good and evil requires the acceptance of the biblical concept of a personal God and a personal devil.

Knowledge of good and evil is the best fruit of the tree of knowledge. "Let each one of us leave every other kind of knowledge," Socrates says at the end of the *Republic*, "and seek and follow one thing only," that is, "to learn and discern between good and evil."

THE DEVIL

The devil is a spirit son of God who was born in the morning of premortal life. He too was an "angel of God . . . he was Lucifer, a son of the morning" and was called Perdition (see D&C 76:26). As with all of Father's children, he was endowed with agency, the power of free choice (see D&C 29:36–37; 93:30). Satan is his Hebrew name (see McConkie, *Mormon Doctrine*, 677).

He chose the evil part from before the world was, and thus it is written of him that he was a liar from the beginning (see Moses 4:3–4). He placed himself in eternal opposition to the divine will. He was "an angel of God" (D&C 76:25) who "became a devil, having sought that which was evil before God" (2 Nephi 2:17).

The Eternal Father had his plan of salvation presented to his spirit children (see Moses 4:2). The general elements of the plan were: that an earth would be made (see Abraham 3:24); that the spirit children would be given tangible bodies and, if faithful in all things, progress to a like status with their Father (see Abraham 3:25–27); and that to effectuate this operation there must needs be a Redeemer (see Abraham 3:27–28; Moses 4:1). When the need for a Redeemer was explained, Satan volunteered to come to earth in this role as the Son of God. "Behold, here am I, send me, I will be thy son." Even in that premortal existence he was in opposition to God's plan. He sought for an amendment. He didn't like the terms upon which salvation was contingent. He wanted to change God's plan. "I will redeem all mankind, that one soul shall not be lost, and surely I will do it; wherefore give me thine honor" (Moses 4:1). His proposed amendment was fundamental. He would deny agency to men. He would guarantee that none would be lost.

"And the Lord said: Whom shall I send? And one answered like unto the Son of Man: Here am I, send me. And another answered and said: Here am I, send me. And the Lord said: I will send the first" (Abraham 3:27). The Son of Man was selected, and Lucifer and his amendment were rejected.

Satan made open war against God.

> Wherefore, because that Satan rebelled against me, and sought to destroy the agency of man, which I, the Lord God, had given him, and also, that I should give unto him mine own power; by the power of mine Only Begotten, I caused that he should be cast down;
>
> And he became Satan, yea, even the devil, the father of all lies, to deceive and to blind men, and to lead them captive at his will, even as many as would not hearken unto my voice. (Moses 4:3–4.)

Because Lucifer rebelled and sought the throne of God, there was war in heaven among the spirit children of God. As we have heretofore noted, such persons are properly designated as angels. John calls them angels in his great revelation.

> And there was war in heaven: Michael and his angels fought against the dragon; and the dragon fought and his angels,
>
> And prevailed not; neither was their place found any more in heaven.
>
> And the great dragon was cast out, that old serpent, called the Devil, and Satan, which deceiveth the whole world: he was

cast out into the earth, and his angels were cast out with him. (Revelation 12:7–9; see also Isaiah 14:12–20.)

"A third part of the hosts of heaven" joined the rebellion. "And they were thrust down, and thus came the devil and his angels" (D&C 29:36–37; see also Revelation 12:4–9; Abraham 3:27–28). Those cast out are denied bodies forever. They are sons of perdition; and, with Lucifer, their foster father, they are in eternal opposition to everything that is right or good.

The devil's purpose is to tempt and entice men to leave the path of truth and walk in darkness. His goal is to get man to worship him: "Behold Satan hath come among the children of men, and tempteth them to worship him; and men have become carnal, sensual, and devilish, and are shut out from the presence of God" (Moses 6:49). He is the enemy of God and the divine order. Jesus said of him, "The enemy that sowed them is the devil" (Matthew 13:39).

One cannot read the Bible without accepting the fact of the devil. He was the tempter of Adam and Eve (see Genesis 3:1–6; 2 Corinthians 11:3). He was the tempter of man. He is a murderer and liar (see Revelation 20:10). Peter presents him as "your adversary the devil" walking about "seeking whom he may devour" (1 Peter 5:8). He struggled mightily to tempt Jesus in a historic earthly confrontation (see Matthew 4:1–11).

Satan has had such success among men in the flesh that he is considered the god of this world. Paul said, "Satan himself is transformed into an angel of light. Therefore it is no great thing if his ministers also be transformed as the ministers of righteousness; whose end shall be according to their works" (2 Corinthians 11:14–15).

At Christ's coming Satan will be bound for one thousand years. He will "deceive the nations no more," but thereafter will "be loosed a little season" (Revelation 20:3). Eventually he "shall not have power over the Saints any more at all" (D&C 88:114).

In eternity, "they who are filthy shall be filthy still; wherefore, they who are filthy are the devil and his angels; and they shall go away into everlasting fire, prepared for them; and their torment is as a lake of fire and brimstone, whose flame ascendeth up forever and ever and has no end" (2 Nephi 9:16).

DEMONS, DEVILS, AND EVIL SPIRITS

Demons, devils, and evil spirits are the beings who followed Lucifer in his war of rebellion in the premortal world. They comprise one-third of those spirit children of the Father who were to come to this earth as a mortal probation (see D&C 29:36–41; Revelation 12:3–9). In New Testament terminology they are "the angels which kept not their first estate" (Jude 1:6), or, as Peter puts it, "God spared not the angels that sinned, but cast them down to hell" (2 Peter 2:4). They are fallen angels and are angels of the devil (see D&C 29:36–38; 2 Nephi 9:9).

In being cast down to earth, they were forever denied physical bodies. Apparently this denial has caused them to seek habitation in the bodies of other persons. Jesus taught the disciples that in his name—that is, by and through "the Holy Priesthood, after the Order of the Son of God" (D&C 107:3)—they could cast out devils. Indeed, he said, "And these signs shall follow them that believe; in my name shall they cast out devils" (Mark 16:17). In this, as in all things, he set the example.

> And there was in their synagogue a man with an unclean spirit; and he cried out,
>
> Saying, Let us alone; what have we to do with thee, thou Jesus of Nazareth? art thou come to destroy us? I know thee who thou art, the Holy One of God.
>
> And Jesus rebuked him, saying, Hold thy peace, and come out of him.
>
> And when the unclean spirit had torn him, and cried with a loud voice, he came out of him.
>
> And they were all amazed, insomuch that they questioned among themselves, saying, What thing is this? what new doctrine is this? for with authority commandeth he even the unclean spirits, and they do obey him.
>
> And immediately his fame spread abroad throughout all the region round about Galilee.

And forthwith, when they were come out of the synagogue, they entered into the house of Simon and Andrew, with James and John.

But Simon's wife's mother lay sick of a fever, and anon they tell him of her.

And he came and took her by the hand, and lifted her up; and immediately the fever left her, and she ministered unto them.

And at even, when the sun did set, they brought unto him all that were diseased, and them that were possessed with devils.

And all the city was gathered together at the door.

And he healed many that were sick of divers diseases, and cast out many devils; and suffered not the devils to speak, because they knew him. (Mark 1:23–34.)

In the foregoing incidents in the ministry of the Lord, Mark is careful to note that some persons were healed from sickness and disease and others were "possessed with devils." No doubt there are many incidents where unsophisticated diagnosis of possession was wrongfully made in lieu of mental illness or other disease. However, Mark makes it clear that Jesus "cast out many devils." This was in addition to healing the sick. Matthew records a time when Jesus cured a "lunatick," but remember, the young man was "sore vexed."

And when they were come to the multitude, there came to him a certain man, kneeling down to him, and saying,

Lord, have mercy on my son: for he is lunatick, and sore vexed: for ofttimes he falleth into the fire, and oft into the water.

And I brought him to thy disciples, and they could not cure him.

Then Jesus answered and said, O faithless and perverse generation, how long shall I be with you? how long shall I suffer you? bring him hither to me.

And Jesus rebuked the devil; and he departed out of him: and the child was cured from that very hour.

Then came the disciples to Jesus apart, and said, Why could not we cast him out?

And Jesus said unto them, Because of your unbelief: for verily I say unto you, If ye have faith as a grain of mustard seed, ye shall say unto this mountain, Remove hence to yonder place; and it shall remove; and nothing shall be impossible unto you.

Howbeit this kind goeth not out but by prayer and fasting. (Matthew 17:14–21.)

This New Testament rendering indicates the unusual amount of faith required to cast out devils. It requires greater faith than most healings. In the cited instance the disciples should have buttressed their faith and prepared themselves by fasting and prayer. One reason for the difficulty of this priestal administration in the name of the Lord is because this is a confrontation between man and the devils. Having been denied a body, there is evidence that they would prefer animal bodies rather than no body at all. Three of the Gospels recite an occasion in which the devils possessing persons requested to be put into swine rather than simply be cast out.

And when he was come to the other side into the country of the Gergesenes, there met him two possessed with devils, coming out of the tombs, exceeding fierce, so that no man might pass by that way.

And, behold, they cried out, saying, What have we to do with thee, Jesus, thou Son of God? art thou come hither to torment us before the time?

And there was a good way off from them an herd of many swine feeding.

So the devils besought him, saying, If thou cast us out, suffer us to go away into the herd of swine.

And he said unto them, Go. And when they were come out, they went into the herd of swine: and, behold, the whole herd of swine ran violently down a steep place into the sea, and perished in the waters. (Matthew 8:28–32; see also Mark 5:13; Luke 8:33.)

Demons are devils. "We are surrounded by demons," the wicked Nephites said, "yea, we are encircled about by angels of him who hath sought to destroy our souls" (Helaman 13:37).

It is written that the devil is the prince of the demons (see Mark 3:22). Evil spirits are devils. They are they of whom it is written, "Satan, which deceiveth the whole world: he was cast out into the earth, and his angels were cast out with him" (Revelation 12:9). Their mission is to make war with the Saints and to destroy the souls of all men.

There are many evil spirits. They enjoy great success. They have been the source of evil philosophical, political, and religious concepts and actions. We are instructed to shun them.

> But ye are commanded in all things to ask of God, who giveth liberally; and that which the Spirit testifies unto you even so I would that ye should do in all holiness of heart, walking uprightly before me, considering the end of your salvation, doing all things with prayer and thanksgiving, that ye may not be seduced by evil spirits, or doctrines of devils, or the commandments of men; for some are of men, and others of devils. (D&C 46:7.)

EXORCISTS

One of the signs that was to follow them who believed the true gospel was, as stated by the Lord, "In my name shall they cast out devils" (Mark 16:17). We have noted several New Testament accounts of the casting out of devils from possessed persons. This has ever been one of the advantages of having the power of God delegated to man; man can act in his name.

In imitation of the true order whereby devils are cast out of people, certain persons called exorcists attempt to cast out devils. Certain priests in the Roman Catholic or Episcopalian churches, for instance, are designated as exorcists. This is attempted by special prescribed prayers, incantations, and adjurations. It is not surprising that there would be such false rituals, inasmuch as the true priesthood ordinance of casting out devils is so documented in the New Testament.

There is a scriptural account of these exorcists. They had seen the Apostle Paul utilize the Holy Melchizedek Priesthood of which he spoke (see Hebrews 3:1; 5:1–10; 7:1–21) in casting out devils in the Lord's name.

> And God wrought special miracles by the hands of Paul:
>
> So that from his body were brought unto the sick handkerchiefs or aprons, and the diseases departed from them, and the evil spirits went out of them.
>
> Then certain of the vagabond Jews, exorcists, took upon them to call over them which had evil spirits the name of the Lord Jesus, saying, We adjure you by Jesus whom Paul preacheth.
>
> And there were seven sons of one Sceva, a Jew, and chief of the priests, which did so.
>
> And the evil spirit answered and said, Jesus I know, and Paul I know; but who are ye?
>
> And the man in whom the evil spirit was leaped on them, and overcame them, and prevailed against them, so that they fled out of that house naked and wounded. (Acts 19:11–16.)

This colorful account indicates that the Apostles, after Christ's ministry, were acting in his name to do what the Lord had directed. Also, it seems to me that we here have a symbolic picture of what is in store for false exorcists.

Exorcists are fraudulent substitutes for legal administrators who are authorized and empowered to act in the name of the Lord.

SPIRITUALISM

Witches, sorcerers, soothsayers, wizards, and spiritualists are persons who attempt, and sometimes apparently attain, communion with departed spirits. The notion that mortals can hold intercourse with spirits of the dead is called spiritualism. It is a false religion.

If it is true that some spiritualists actually make contact with spirits, we should be concerned as to what spirits are available for such practice. The first spirits obviously available are the spirits who were cast out of heaven onto the earth for rebellion. As we have heretofore documented, these spirits are devils and demons. Spirits of persons who have died who would concern themselves with these spiritual jags would be spirits of depraved persons who, because of their wickedness in the flesh, find themselves in the dominion of the devil. "Righteous spirits would have nothing but contempt and pity for the attempts of mediums to make contact with them" (McConkie, *Mormon Doctrine*, 759).

When God had departed from Saul and Saul could get no answers to his prayers, he compounded his sins by going to the witch of Endor. The King James Version of the Bible indicates that the deceased prophet Samuel talked to Saul. Under inspiration from God the Prophet Joseph Smith corrects this account in the Inspired Version of the Bible. The witch had "a familiar spirit," that is, apparently could commune with evil spirits. However, she did not bring up Samuel, nor did Saul converse with Samuel. The witch said that she saw Samuel and said, "These are the words of Samuel to Saul." This is a technique used by mediums today, who purportedly contact the spirits and report the messages. If they contact a devil, they contact a person of considerable knowledge with some insight into the future. The righteous Samuel was not cavorting with witches in the corrected account (see Inspired Version, 1 Samuel 28).

Isaiah gave instructions relative to going to spiritualists and the falsity of spiritualism. He indicated that the prophets lead to God, not others.

> Behold, I and the children whom the Lord hath given me are for signs and for wonders in Israel from the Lord of hosts, which dwelleth in mount Zion.
> And when they shall say unto you, Seek unto them that have familiar spirits, and unto wizards that peep, and that mutter: should not a people seek unto their God? for the living to the dead? (Isaiah 8:18–19.)

The Prophet Joseph Smith rendered the salient sentence: " . . . should not a people seek unto their God? for the living to hear from the dead?" (Inspired Version, Isaiah 8:19).

The Lord sought to keep his ancient covenant people from the evils of spiritualism. The law stated:

When thou art come into the land which the Lord thy God giveth thee, thou shalt not learn to do after the abominations of those nations.

There shall not be found among you any one that maketh his son or his daughter to pass through the fire, or that useth divination, or an observer of times, or an enchanter, or a witch,

Or a charmer, or a consulter with familiar spirits, or a wizard, or a necromancer.

For all that do these things are an abomination unto the Lord: and because of these abominations the Lord thy God doth drive them out from before thee. (Deuteronomy 18:9–12.)

Such activity was considered such a serious wrongdoing in ancient Israel that it carried the death penalty. "A man also or woman that hath a familiar spirit, or that is a wizard, shall surely be put to death" (Leviticus 20:27; see also Exodus 22:18). At best, it is foolishness to trifle with powers about which we know little. It is also a scripturally condemned practice.

DISCERNING OF SPIRITS

Some angels are on God's errand; some are from the realm of Satan himself. "Believe not every spirit," John counseled, "but try the spirits whether they are of God: because many false prophets are gone out into the world" (1 John 4:1). The problem that most men have is to discern the spirits so that they may know what is of God and what is not.

Try the spirits. But how? By what test can it be known whether they are of God or the devil? If a messenger appears from the unseen world, how can one know if it is a good spirit or an evil spirit? When there are trances, tongues, visions, or apparent miracles, are they from above or below? When a doctrine is proclaimed or a religion preached, how shall we know whether it is true or false?

To some extent everyone is given a gift of the spirit of discernment. This ability is conferred upon people generally by operations of the Light of Christ (see Moroni 7:12–18). In addition to this universal gift, faithful Saints receive special discerning power through revelation from the Holy Ghost (see D&C 63:41).

The Apostle Paul gives instruction concerning spiritual gifts. He specifically lists the "discerning of spirits" as a gift of the Spirit (see 1 Corinthians 12:10). Modern revelation says, "to some is given, by the Spirit of God . . . the discerning of spirits" (D&C 46:17, 23). The only sure way to distinguish between good and evil (Moroni 7:12–18), between righteousness and wickedness (D&C 101:95; Malachi 3:18; 3 Nephi 24:18), or between evil spirits and those spirits that manifest the things of God is by the promptings of the Holy Ghost. There is no perfect operation of the power of discernment without revelation from God. That is why the righteous are given the gift of the Holy Ghost (see Joseph F. Smith, *Gospel Doctrine*, 61).

We might well look to the Prophet Joseph Smith as an example without peer in the matter of manifestations and angels. "We may look for angels and receive their ministrations," he said, "but we are to try the spirits and prove them, for it is often the case that men make a mistake in regard to these things. . . . When you see a vision, pray for the interpretation; if you get not this, shut it up; there must be certainty in this matter. . . . Lying spirits are going forth in the earth. There will be great manifestations of spirits, both false and true" (*TPJS*, 161). He gives us the key to the whole matter: "The devil may appear as an angel of light. *Ask God to reveal it* . . . if it be of . . . God, He will . . . make it manifest" (ibid., 162). The following is abstracted from one of the Prophet's lengthy statements on the subject.

> "Try the spirits," but what by? . . .
>
> One great evil is, that men are ignorant of the nature of spirits; their power, laws, government, intelligence, etc., and imagine that when there is anything like power, revelation, or vision manifested, that it must be of God. . . . Is there any intelligence communicated? Are the curtains of heaven withdrawn, or the purposes of God developed? . . .
>
> Every one of these professes to be competent to try his neighbor's spirit, but no one can try his own, and what is the

reason? Because they have not a key to unlock, no rule where-with to measure, and no criterion whereby they can test it. . . . We answer that no man can do this without the Priesthood, and having a knowledge of the laws by which spirits are governed; for as no man knows the spirit of the devil, and his power and influence, but by possessing intelligence which is more than human, and having unfolded through the medium of the Priesthood the mysterious operations of his devices; . . .

A man must have the discerning of spirits before he can drag into daylight this hellish influence and unfold it unto the world in all its soul-destroying, diabolical, and horrid colors; for nothing is a greater injury to the children of men than to be under the influence of a false spirit when they think they have the Spirit of God. Thousands have felt the influence of its terrible power and baneful effects. Long pilgrimages have been undertaken, penances endured, and pain, misery and ruin have followed in their train; nations have been convulsed, kingdoms overthrown, provinces laid waste, and blood, carnage and desolation are habiliments in which it has been clothed.

As we have noticed before, the great difficulty lies in the ignorance of the nature of spirits, of the laws by which they are governed, and the signs by which they may be known; if it requires the Spirit of God to know the things of God; and the spirit of the devil can only be unmasked through that medium, then it follows as a natural consequence that unless some person or persons have a communication, or revelation from God, unfolding to them the operation of the spirit, they must eternally remain ignorant of these principles; for I contend that if one man cannot understand these things but by the Spirit of God, ten thousand men cannot; it is alike out of the reach of the wis-dom of the learned, the tongue of the eloquent, the power of the mighty. And we shall at last have to come to this conclusion, whatever we may think of revelation, that without it we can neither know nor understand anything of God, or the devil; and however unwilling the world may be to acknowledge this principle, it is evident from the multifarious creeds and notions concerning this matter that they understand nothing of this principle, and it is equally as plain that without a divine com-munication they must remain in ignorance. (*TPJS*, 203–206.)

This dissertation is so like Joseph Smith. He has had the experience. He doesn't argue. He speaks as one having authority.

He puts the truth simply. "And we shall at last have to come to this conclusion, whatever we may think of revelation, that without it we can neither know nor understand anything of God, or the devil."

There are two spirits abroad in the earth. One is of God; the other is of the devil. The spirit that is of God leads to light, truth, freedom, and every good thing. The spirit that is of Lucifer leads to darkness, error, bondage, and every evil thing. They are at enmity one with another, with conflict between them. The "power" of one is the "spirit" "that now worketh in the children of disobedience" (Ephesians 2:2). The other is "revealed" by the Spirit of God. And no man knoweth "the things of God" but by "the Spirit of God" (1 Corinthians 2:11).

ANGEL OF THE BOTTOMLESS PIT

John uses the expression "the angel of the bottomless pit" (Revelation 9:11) to describe Satan. He refers particularly to Satan's status as king of hell, for Satan is the ruling authority over those cast into the pit that is hell.

The bottomless pit is the depths of hell. It is not a literal pit without a bottom; such would be a contradiction in terms. It is an attempt in imperfect language to convey the idea of the intensity of the sufferings of those who go to hell (see Revelation 9:1–2; 11:7; 17:8; 20:1–3).

ACKNOWLEDGMENT OF GOD

The Father and the Son are the objects of all true worship. "Thou shalt worship the Lord thy God, and him only shalt thou serve" (Matthew 4:10; Luke 4:8; see also Exodus 34:14; D&C 20:17–19; Mosiah 18:25). No one can worship the Father without worshiping the Son. "All men should honour the Son, even as they honour the Father. He that honoureth not the Son honoureth not the Father which hath sent him" (John 5:23). Worship consists in paying divine honors to Diety.

"Give unto the Lord the glory due unto his name; worship the Lord in the beauty of holiness" (Psalm 29:2). There is no true worship without "the beauty of holiness," that is, personal righteousness. Obedience is the true measure of true worship. "But in vain they do worship me, teaching for doctrines the commandments of men" (Matthew 15:9).

Part of worship is the showing of obeisance. "All things bow in humble reverence" before the Father (D&C 76:93; see also Genesis 24:52; Numbers 22:31).

It is written that Christ has power over the devil's angels (see Mark 5:8; Matthew 8:29). They know Jesus (Acts 19:15). They tremble before the Lord's mighty power: "Thou believest that there is one God; thou doest well: the devils also believe, and tremble" (James 2:19). The devils, being evil, are incapable of true worship. However, they are under the necessity of acknowledging God and giving obeisance to him. They are subject to him and well know it. They whined as he cast them out, "What have we to do with thee, Jesus, thou Son of God? art thou come hither to torment us before the time?" (Matthew 8:29).

*Could you really
accept a religion as
the true way of God
without God's personal
messengers in it?*

MINISTERING OF ANGELS

Evidence proves that there are angels. In point of fact, there is no evidence to the contrary. The best evidence of the skeptic is that it can be proved that the vast majority of people have not had personal experience with angels; however, the fact that most people have not seen angels is not a valid argument that angels don't exist. It is rather like attempting to prove a case by presenting a myriad of witnesses who are totally unfamiliar with the facts of the case, having neither seen nor participated in the situation personally. Many creditable witnesses have seen and heard and have been ministered to by angels. Any serious, believing perusal of the scriptures establishes beyond any reasonable doubt the existence of angels.

We have heretofore examined who angels are, their types and kinds, their functions and purposes, the several most prominent angels, and fallen angels. Angels are. They exist and have functions and purposes. Unless one simply rejects the testimony of Jesus, the prophets and apostles, ancient and modern, and without other evidence simply assumes the contrary position, one must accept the fact that there are angels.

The legitimate question, it seems to me, is not whether there are angels; but, assuming that angels do exist, what has this to do with us? So there are angels? So what? Let us consider this important question.

I was once leading a tour of visitors on Temple Square in Salt Lake City, Utah. I took the visitors, in their minds' eyes, back to the arid desert basin that was the Salt Lake Valley prior to the arrival of the Mormon pioneers. Hardly a tree was there. The ground was baked so hard that the first two plows put to the sod were broken. A stream had to be dammed and the land irrigated before the ground could be broken up for planting. But the faith of the pioneers and the benevolence of a kind Providence eventually made the desert blossom. My listeners were encompassed about with a cloud of witnesses. They were standing in the midst of a society that evidenced the refining influence of the true gospel of Christ. I remember quoting the Savior's test of those professing to be bearers of the truth, "Wherefore by their fruits ye shall know them" (Matthew 7:20). There were far too many good fruits here for falsehoods.

An honest worldly query was made: "We like what we see. You have met the Master's test. The kingdom of God seems to be here. Why make it incredible by predicating it on angels? Why must such a rational and beautiful approach to religion and life be based on the administration of angels?"

Maybe it was my legal training that prompted an answer in the form of a question: "Could you really accept a religion as the true way of God without God's personal messengers in it?"

SOUND REASONS

"Come now, and let us reason together, saith the Lord" (Isaiah 1:18). "Bring forth your strong reasons" (Isaiah 41:21), the scriptures enjoin. Peter, the chief of the original Apostles, counsels, "Be ready always to give an answer to every man that asketh you a reason of the hope that is in you" (1 Peter 3:1). We are encouraged to have reason and logical structure for our doctrines and beliefs. Clearly this lends stability to our faith. Let us reason.

It is admitted that The Church of Jesus Christ of Latter-day Saints has a remarkably efficient organization. The institutional Church has been likened to the most effective of earthly armies. In its organizational chart the lines of authority are clear. They flow from the president of the Church, through appropriate priesthood leadership, directly to the head of every family. The various helps and governments (see 1 Corinthians 12:28) are an earthly approximation of God's perfect order of things. Basically the Church organization has been the same in all ages. The same organization that existed in the primitive church prevails now (see Article of Faith 6). Whenever the Church has been truly established on the earth, apostolic power has been manifest. In such periods there have always been prophets, evangelists, pastors, and teachers (see Ephesians 4:11–14).

The genius of the organization is not found in its flow charts and lines of communication and the like. It is found in the revelation from the heavens, whence the organization comes. Through modern revelation, it ideally suits the contemporary needs of the people amid changing circumstances. If we are to find the true religion, we must find the religion that was instituted of God for the benefit of man.

How would a religion be instituted of God? By revelation from him. As used in the gospel, "*revelation* signifies the making known of divine truth by communication from the heavens" (James E. Talmage, *Articles of Faith*, 296). Revelation comes from God to men in various appointed ways, according to the will of the Almighty. One way that he has ordained is that angels are sent from his presence to do his will. This cannot be contradicted by logic. The Church of Jesus Christ of Latter-day Saints enjoys an unassailable position. It is a *revealed* religion. God has seen fit to reveal the way to perfection, including the necessary helps and governments for the benefit of man, by way of angelic administrations.

In this matter of sound reasoning, we stand alone. The Roman Catholic and Greek Orthodox churches look to tradition for much of their footing. History's judgment of them is harsh. It is historically clear that the prophesied great falling away has taken place (see 2 Thessalonians 2:1–12). The Protestants, inspired as their revolution was, are not in a sound logical position. If the mother church were apostate, as they claimed, whence do they get their authority? They could reform, yes. But how does one become a legal administrator when the one from whom one is rebelling has lost authority? It was the Lord himself who foretold the perplexities, the calamities, and the apostate wickedness of the days in which we live (see Matthew 24; Mark 13; Luke 21).

By virtue of the ministrations of God's messengers, the position of "the only true and living church upon the face of the whole earth" (D&C 1:30) is secure. We should not shy away from this position of strength. We should take comfort in it. Among the religions of the world today, we stand at the head in our claimed foundation.

Jesus commended Peter for his testimony, saying, "Flesh and blood hath not revealed it unto thee, but my Father which is in heaven, . . . and upon this rock I will build my church" (Matthew 16:17–18). Commenting on this statement, the Prophet Joseph Smith said, "What rock? Revelation" (*TPJS*, 274).

Consider the reasoning and validity of this argument. Jesus himself was "called of God an high priest after the order of Melchisedec" (Hebrews 5:10). "And no man taketh this honour unto himself, but he that is called of God, as was Aaron" (Hebrews 5:4). That is, by prophecy (see Exodus 28:1) and the laying on of hands (see Numbers 27:18). Jesus chose and ordained Peter and his associates (John 15:16). Jesus conferred upon Peter the same priesthood, the order of Melchizedek, that he himself had forever (Hebrews 5:6). Peter referred to it as "an holy priesthood" and "a royal priesthood" that constituted certain ones as "the people of God" (1 Peter 2:5, 9–10).

The Lord further gave to Peter and the ancient Apostles "the keys of the kingdom of heaven" (Matthew 16:19; see also Matthew 18:18). Those so endowed have power to govern all the earthly affairs of the kingdom of God and to direct the administration of all the ordinances of salvation for worthy recipients (see D&C 35:25; 42:69; 65; 90:2–3; 97:14; 115:19).

There was a time appointed in which all things were to be restored "which God hath spoken by the mouth of all his holy prophets since the world began" (Acts 3:21). All things are to be gathered together in one in Christ (see Ephesians 1:10). Gospel restoration is accomplished in the same way in which the gospel was first revealed. Angelic ministrants are sent from heaven to declare it; God declares its truth by his own voice; and the gift of the Holy Ghost is given to men (see Moses 4:58).

Peter, James, and John, messengers from God, came to Joseph Smith and Oliver Cowdery and restored the priesthood Jesus had given them and all of the keys needed to exalt men in the highest heaven (see D&C 27:12–13; 110:11–16; 128:20–21).

All of the people of God who have subsequently been called of God as was Aaron can trace their line of authority to Jesus Christ in a few steps.[1]

This is strong reason for the hope which is in us.

This same compelling logic applies to each step of the restoration of the gospel. For instance, the gathering of Israel has been promised as part of the dispensation of the fulness of times (see 1 Nephi 15:19–20; 2 Nephi 3:13–24; D&C 45:17; Acts 1:6). This means that scattered remnants of Israel will be converted to the true church (see 2 Nephi 9:2; 30:5; Mormon 9:36) and that Israel will be assembled to Zion or Jerusalem. (See Article of Faith 10; D&C 110:11; 2 Nephi 25:11; 30:8; Mormon 5:14.)

Moses held the keys to the leading and gathering and teaching of Israel. Those were the special powers and endowments that rested with the kingdom in his day. On 3 April 1836, Moses appeared to Joseph Smith and Oliver Cowdery and committed to them the keys of the gathering of Israel and the leading of the ten tribes from the land of the north (see D&C 110:11). By virtue of the restoration of these keys, men are now authorized to use the priesthood for these great purposes.

The prophet Elias holds "the keys of bringing to pass the restoration of all things spoken by the mouth of all the holy prophets since the world began, concerning the last days" (D&C 27:6; see also D&C 77:9, 14–15; Matthew 17:11; Mark 7:12). These keys have been restored and conferred upon man. Such things as have not already been revealed will be made known "in due time" (see D&C 132:45; 2 Nephi 25:11; 30:8; Mormon 5:14).

Malachi prophesied that Elijah would return before the great and dreadful day of the Lord.

> Behold, I will send you Elijah the prophet before the coming of the great and dreadful day of the Lord:
>
> And he shall turn the heart of the fathers to the children, and the heart of the children to their fathers, lest I come and smite the earth with a curse. (Malachi 4:5–6.)

In fulfillment of this Old Testament prophecy Elijah came to Joseph Smith and Oliver Cowdery in the Kirtland Temple on 3 April 1836 and conferred upon them the keys of the sealing power (see D&C 110:13–16).

It is because Elijah has come in this dispensation that the fulness of salvation is again available for the living and the dead. He "was the last Prophet that held the keys of the Priesthood" in ancient Israel, the Prophet Joseph Smith said. His latter-day mission was to "restore the authority and deliver the keys of the Priesthood, in order that all the ordinances may be attended to in righteousness. . . . Why send Elijah? Because he holds the keys of the authority to administer in all the ordinances of the Priesthood; and without the authority is given, the ordinances could not be administered in righteousness" (*TPJS*, 172).

"The spirit, power, and calling of Elijah," the Prophet Joseph Smith also taught, "is, that ye have power to hold the key of the revelations, ordinances, oracles, powers and endowments of the fulness of the Melchizedek Priesthood and of the kingdom of God on the earth; and to receive, obtain, and perform all the ordinances belonging to the kingdom of God, even unto the turning of the hearts of the fathers unto the children, and the hearts of the children unto the fathers, even those who are in heaven" (*TPJS*, 337).

In all of this we not only deal from a position of strength, but it must also logically follow that man's very salvation is contingent upon angelic administrations.

If, indeed, the Lord gave something to Peter, James, and John that was necessary for man's salvation, then it must needs to be that the same be given to man in our day, if man is to enjoy the same result in our day.

So also with Moses.

If the prophecies of the scriptures are to be fulfilled, Elias and Elijah must come. It is the unique position of The Church of Jesus Christ of Latter-day Saints that they *have* come. Angelic ministration is vital and necessary to the restoration of the fulness of the gospel. This is sound reasoning. This is compelling argument. The Church is based on the truth.

"How shall God come to the rescue of this generation?" the Prophet Joseph Smith asked. "He will send Elijah the prophet. . . . Elijah shall reveal the covenants to seal the hearts of the fathers to the children, and the children to the fathers. The anointing and sealing is to be called, elected, and made sure" (*TPJS*, 323).

COMPOSITE ANGEL

It has been heretofore noted that certain of God's messengers have been prophesied of in times past. Thus, their visitations have been in fulfillment of prophecy. Perhaps the most noteworthy prophecy of angelic administration in traditional Christendom was made by John the Revelator. Foreseeing the final great restoration of the gospel, the ancient Apostle wrote:

> And I saw another angel fly in the midst of heaven, having the everlasting gospel to preach unto them that dwell on the earth, and to every nation, and kindred, and tongue, and people,
> Saying with a loud voice, Fear God, and give glory to him; for the hour of his judgment is come: and worship him that made heaven, and earth, and the sea, and the fountains of waters. (Revelation 4:6–7.)

Many angels were to participate in the events envisioned as necessary to complete the restoration. "This angel of the restoration was a *composite angel*, meaning that a number of angels were destined to participate in the events which necessarily must take place to complete the restoration" (McConkie, *Mormon Doctrine*, 635). The Angel Moroni is usually more particularly associated with the fulfillment of this prophecy. This is because he effected the restoration of the Book of Mormon wherein the doctrines of the true gospel are recorded (see D&C 133:36–40; 135:3). Therefore, the "everlasting gospel" is restored. However, John the Baptist, Peter, James, and John, Michael, Raphael, Gabriel, Elias, Moses, Elijah, and "divers angels" (D&C 128:21) all came in fulfillment of this promise and restored priesthood and priesthood keys. It was in this way that the gospel was made operative in the lives of men (see D&C 13; 27:12–13; 88:103–104; 110:11–16).

The Apostle Paul makes the preceptive observation that the gospel consists of two parts: the word and the power (see 1 Thessalonians 1:5). Moroni brought that major portion of the word which is found in the Book of Mormon and which records the saving truths of the way to salvation; the other angels restored power. Moroni brought the message or word; the other angels brought the power of priesthood. All of this has been accomplished.

Yet the work of the angel of the restoration is not complete yet. Part of his work is in a postmillennial setting. This great prophecy of the ministration of angels has not been fully fulfilled. There will yet be other angelic administrants before "the hour of his judgment is come" (D&C 88:103–104).

INFORMATION GAINED FROM ANGELS

One of the important aspects of the ministration of angels is that we learn from them. The great King Benjamin delivered one of the most truth-laden sermons recorded in the scriptures. For more than two pages he simply quotes what an angel told him (see Mosiah 3). We have noted that one of the functions of angels is to teach. One can be sure one is getting at the heart of the matter if the word comes from a true messenger from God. Thus the essence of the angelic discourse to King Benjamin was that "salvation was, and is, and is to come, in and through the atoning blood of Christ, the Lord Omnipotent" (Mosiah 3:18). We are indebted to the angels for cutting through the irrelevant and setting our course squarely on the object of all true worship.

The revelation of John the Revelator, with its wealth of information, was given "by his angel unto his servant John" (Revelation 1:1). That book sheds forth a blaze of light on gospel understanding. Through this angel we have revealed a guide in overcoming the world and gaining salvation. He speaks with a voice that makes clear the mysteries of the kingdom. He tells of the restoration of eternal truth. Could anyone with spiritual discernment ask if angels are really relevant? What is more relevant than happiness and fulfillment here and salvation hereafter?

Let us examine two verses to see what insight we can gain to the eternal scheme of things. John records that he sees the Saints and angels singing praises to Christ after he comes in his glory.

> And they sung a new song, saying, Thou art worthy to take the book, and to open the seals thereof: for thou wast slain, and hast redeemed us to God by thy blood out of every kindred, and tongue, and people, and nation;
> And hast made us unto our God kings and priests: and we shall reign on the earth.
> And I beheld, and I heard the voice of many angels . . . (Revelation 5:9–11.)

These are saved beings who are singing. They are praising God for redeeming them. Full redemption is a blessing reserved for the Saints (see D&C 35:26; 45:46; 133:52). They are gathered out of every nation. The appeal of truth is universal, and this choir is made up of people from every nation. God had made them kings and priests; that is, they had enjoyed the ordinances of the holy temples while on earth.

What do we learn from this description of this angelic choir? We learn that before Christ comes in his glory, there will be converted and endowed Saints in every nation. All of this teaches us that there is much to be done in spreading the gospel over the earth before the coming of the Son of Man.

All of this is made known to us through the ministration of

angels. We are indebted to angels for much of our understanding in gospel scholarship.

KEYS OF THE MINISTERING OF ANGELS

The power and authority of the lesser, or Aaronic Priesthood, is to hold the keys of the ministering of angels (see D&C 84:26–27).

This means that the Aaronic Priesthood opens the door to all that we have discussed relative to the ministering of angels. Quite literally this means that those holding the Aaronic Priesthood are in a position to have angels minister unto them. Inasmuch as this is the express potential of such a priesthood bearer, one is not fully enjoying his office and calling in the absence of such a wondrous experience. Wilford Woodruff, for instance, said: "I had the administration of angels while holding the office of a priest" (*Discourses of Wilford Woodruff*, 298).

The scriptures reiterate that the keys of the ministering of angels have to do with the Aaronic Priesthood. On 15 May 1829, the angelic visitant, John the Baptist, came to Joseph Smith and Oliver Cowdery and, averring that he acted under the direction of Peter, James, and John, conferred upon them the Aaronic Priesthood, saying:

> Upon you my fellow servants, in the name of Messiah I confer the Priesthood of Aaron, which holds the keys of the ministering of angels, and of the gospel of repentance, and of baptism by immersion for the remission of sins; and this shall never be taken again from the earth, until the sons of Levi do offer again an offering unto the Lord in righteousness. (D&C 13.)

In a revelation given six years later, the Lord said:

> The power and authority of the lesser, or Aaronic Priesthood, is to hold the keys of the ministering of angels, and to administer in outward ordinances, the letter of the gospel, the baptism of repentance for the remission of sins, agreeable to the covenants and commandments. (D&C 107:20.)

Historically angels have to do with the lesser priesthood. Ancient Israel was given the lesser priesthood to administer the lesser law (see Hebrews 7:12; Inspired Version, Exodus 34:1–2). This priesthood was conferred upon Aaron and his sons after him (see Exodus 28–30; Leviticus 1:11; 3:2; 13:2; Numbers 18). It was conferred upon substantially the whole house of Levi who were between thirty and fifty years of age (see Numbers 4:3). Aaron and his sons after him held the keys of the Aaronic Priesthood. The rest of the Levites held the Aaronic Priesthood (see Hebrews 7:5) but did not hold the keys of this ministry. Moses records the function of an angel incident to this ancient ministry.

> And the Lord said unto Moses, Depart, and go up hence, thou and the people which thou hast brought up out of the land of Egypt, unto the land which I sware unto Abraham, to Isaac, and to Jacob, saying, Unto thy seed will I give it:
>
> And I will send an angel before thee; and I will drive out the Canaanite, the Amorite, and the Hittite, and the Perizzite, the Hivite, and the Jebusite:
>
> Unto a land flowing with milk and honey: for I will not go up in the midst of thee; for thou art a stiffnecked people: lest I consume thee in the way.
>
> And when the people heard these evil tidings, they mourned: and no man did put on him his ornaments. (Exodus 33:1–4.)

The Priesthood of Aaron "is called the lesser priesthood . . . because it is an appendage to the greater, or the Melchizedek Priesthood, and has power in administering outward ordinances" (D&C 107:14). In commenting upon this passage, a modern scholar says, "Though it is a lesser priesthood, it is yet one of great majesty and power. It holds 'the keys of the ministering of angels,' meaning that those who hold it and are faithful have the key whereby they can open the door to the receipt of visitations from heavenly messengers" (McConkie, *Mormon Doctrine*, 11).

Perfection does not come by this order of the priesthood. "If therefore perfection were by the Levitical priesthood, (for under it the people received the law,) what further need was there that another priest should rise after the order of Melchisedec, and not be called after the order of Aaron?" (Hebrews 7:11). However, the keys of the administering of angels have been given. Insofar as we do not use these offered blessings, we default in our priestly prerogatives.

MINISTRY OF ANGELS AND THE PRESENCE OF GOD

The Lord has ordained the lesser priesthood and its concomitant blessings of ministering of angels so that we might prepare ourselves for the higher priesthood and its concomitant blessings of his personal ministrations to us.

In a revelation given through Joseph Smith, the Prophet, at Kirtland, Ohio, on 24 February 1834, the Lord said:

> Therefore, let not your hearts faint, for I say not unto you as I said unto your fathers: Mine angel shall go up before you, but not my presence.
> But I say unto you: Mine angels shall go up before you, and also my presence, and in time ye shall possess the goodly land. (D&C 103:19–20.)

Ancient Israel was given "an angel before thee," but not the presence of God; "for I will not go up in the midst of thee . . ." (Exodus 33:3). Modern Israel was given the promise that "angels shall go up before you, and also my presence . . ." (D&C 103:20).

As the Aaronic Priesthood holds the keys of the ministering of angels, so the Melchizedek Priesthood holds "the key of the knowledge of God" (D&C 84:19) and "of all the spiritual blessings of the church" in that the holders of that priesthood may "have the heavens opened unto them" and "enjoy the communion and presence of God the Father, and Jesus the mediator of the new covenant" (D&C 107:18–19).

What do angels have to do with us? The Aaronic Priesthood and the Melchizedek Priesthood were restored to the earth in our day by angels (see D&C 13; 27:12–13). Our salvation is contingent upon them. The priesthood of the ministry of angels is to prepare us for the priesthood of our Lord's personal ministry to us.

It is the means to have "another comforter" and have "our abode" with the God of Heaven (see John 14).

WHAT ANGELS WILL NOT DO

Angels do not attend men unless there is need. It is not their errand to satisfy idle curiosity. We have no scriptural accounts of any angels doing any service for man that man could have done without the help of the angel. With the ample precedents available for examination, we can establish this principle as the order of heaven.

A preeminent Latter-day Saint scripturalist and former Church president, Joseph Fielding Smith, said: "It is contrary to the law of God for the heavens to be opened and messengers to come to do anything for man that man can do for himself" (*Doctrines of Salvation*, 1:196).

Angels do what is essential, and they do not do what man could do without them. When Moroni came to the youthful Joseph Smith, he told him that ancient records were in the Hill Cumorah and that he was going to turn them over to Joseph. Joseph was given instruction for four years; then he received the records and was required to translate. Why didn't Moroni translate? He knew the language, and it would have been no trouble for him to do it, whereas Joseph didn't know the language. It was a difficult assignment, but not an impossible one. Joseph could translate by the gift and power of God, which is in accordance with all angelic precedents. Angels do not do for us what we can do for ourselves. Joseph Smith followed the scriptural pattern.

Take, for instance, the case of Peter and Cornelius. Cornelius was a devout man who sought the Lord, and an angel appeared. The angel did not say, "Cornelius, the gospel has been restored, and since you are a good man and you believe, I will take you out and baptize you." He told Cornelius where he could go and be taught and have the saving ordinance performed. Then the angelic messenger went to Peter. He taught Peter and directed him so he would know what to do when Cornelius came to him.

After sending Cornelius to Peter, the angel made sure that Peter would properly attend to the baptism. The angel did only that which was essential—that is all (see Acts 10).

When the Savior appeared as a heavenly messenger to Saul and stopped him in his mad course of persecution of the Saints, what did he do? He sent him to find the righteous Ananias. This mortal legal administrator would tell him what to do. Then he sent word to Ananias about Paul and told Ananias he had a mission for Paul. He told Ananias to find Paul and do what was necessary for him to have salvation (see Acts 9:1–18; 22:6–16). This is the way the Lord works. It is the order of the heavens.

To have a proper and correct understanding of the doings of angels, it is necessary to know what they will not do, even as it is necessary to know what they have done and will do. This is definition by exclusion.

The heavenly messengers do only what we cannot do for ourselves. "The only reason that Jesus Christ became the Redeemer of the world, and came here to atone for the transgressions of man, was that we could not redeem ourselves. It required an infinite atonement, as the Book of Mormon says. He came to do what no one else could do" (Smith, *Doctrines of Salvation*, 1:196; see also 2 Nephi 9:7).

---

1. For instance, the line of priesthood authority for the author is:

OSCAR W. McCONKIE JR. was ordained to the office of an elder in the Melchizedek Priesthood October 22, 1944, by Oscar W. McConkie Sr.

OSCAR W. McCONKIE SR. was ordained by Rulon S. Wells November 7, 1909.

RULON S. WELLS was ordained by Brigham Young October 22, 1875.

BRIGHAM YOUNG was ordained an apostle February 14, 1835, under the hands of the three witnesses of the Book of Mormon: Oliver Cowdery, David Whitmer, and Martin Harris, "who were blessed by the laying on of hands of the Presidency [Joseph Smith Jr., Sidney Rigdon, and Frederick G. Williams]" to "choose the Twelve Apostles." (*History of the Church*, 2:187; see also D&C 18:37.)

JOSEPH SMITH JR. was ordained by Peter, James, and John in 1829.

PETER, JAMES, AND JOHN were ordained by the Lord Jesus Christ.

*One
man
and God
make a
majority*

ANGELS AND US

Let's personalize this discussion on angels. It does appear from the scriptures that from Adam to the present time, whenever men have had sufficient faith, angels have ministered to them. The pattern and examples are before us; so is the precept. It is an unvarying principle. Moroni quoted his father, Mormon, as saying:

> Have miracles ceased? . . .
> . . . Behold I say unto you, Nay; neither have angels ceased to minister unto the children of men.
> For behold, they are subject unto him, to minister according to the word of his command, showing themselves unto them of strong faith and a firm mind in every form of godliness. . . .
> Or have angels ceased to appear unto the children of men? . . .
> Behold I say unto you, Nay; for it is by faith that . . . angels appear and minister unto men; wherefore, if these things have ceased wo be unto the children of men, for it is because of unbelief, and all is vain. (Moroni 7:27, 29–30, 36–37.)

By precept and example we understand that angels minister to faithful servants.

David praised the Lord for this principle. "The angel of the Lord encampeth round about them that fear him, and delivereth them. . . . O fear the Lord, ye his Saints: for there is no want to them that fear him" (Psalm 34:7, 9).

King David knew what he was talking about. He had

experienced the angelic forces of God in his behalf. In inspired song he sang: "He hath delivered my soul in peace from the battle that was against me: for there were many with me" (Psalm 55:18). This is an apparent reference to the Assyrian invasion of Judah wherein the righteous troops were encouraged:

> Be strong and courageous, be not afraid nor dismayed for the King of Assyria, nor for all the multitude that is with him: for there be more with us than with him:
> With him is an arm of flesh; but with us is the Lord our God to help us, and to fight our battles. (2 Chronicles 32:7–8.)

One trouble is that we do not enjoy the joint effort that we otherwise might have. One of the purposes of this essay is to help us recognize our possibilities. When we see what angels have done with others, we may open our eyes.

There is a great Old Testament incident wherein the man of God saw the angelic hosts marshaled in favor of the forces of righteousness. By intercessory prayer the prophet was able to open the eyes of the people, and they became aware of the strength of their position. They saw that there were more that were for them than there were that were against them.

> Therefore sent he thither horses, and chariots, and a great host: and they came by night, and compassed the city about.
> And when the servant of the man of God was risen early, and gone forth, behold, an host compassed the city both with horses and chariots. And his servant said unto him, Alas, my master! how shall we do?
> And he answered, Fear not: for they that be with us are more than they that be with them.
> And Elisha prayed, and said, Lord, I pray thee, open his eyes, that he may see. And the Lord opened the eyes of the young man; and he saw: and, behold, the mountain was full of horses and chariots of fire round about Elisha. (2 Kings 6:14–17.)

Since God is no respecter of persons, we can safely assume that he will treat us as he treated Elisha's men. It is as important in our lives, as it was in theirs, to know that "they that be with us are more than they that be with them."

In preparing this manuscript, I initially selected several occurrences, all within my jurisdiction in terms of area and time and church administration, events either personally witnessed or faithfully recounted to me by the participants, so that we, too, may see. In my personal, limited stewardship, I have been able to record many instances of the ministering of angels now. These were not hearsay, but were first-party testimony. Upon mature consideration it is my judgment not to permit a listing of such intensely personal and sacred experiences while the participants are still with us. It seems wisdom to me not to name buildings after living heroes.

To avoid any hazards in adding to the burden of sensitive, spiritually attuned, living witnesses, I have determined to make my point by retelling some verified, heretofore-published accountings of persons who established, in the entirety of their lives, a reputation for honesty and integrity and faithfulness.

We are not alone. One man and God make a majority. There are many with us.

WILFORD WOODRUFF

Consider first the testimony of the fourth president of The Church of Jesus Christ of Latter-day Saints, Wilford Woodruff. This statement was made in the solemnity of a general conference of the Church in the Salt Lake Tabernacle on Sunday afternoon, 10 October 1880. It has to do with the spirits of just men made perfect. The spirits of certain persons who have left their bodies in death and who reside in the spirit world are angels. Perusal of the modern and ancient records indicates that most angelic visitants are of this kind.

> I believe the eyes of the heavenly hosts are over this people; I believe they are watching the elders of Israel, the prophets and apostles and men who are called to bear off this kingdom. I believe they watch over us all with great interest.

I will here make a remark concerning my own feelings. After the death of Joseph Smith I saw and conversed with him many times in my dreams in the night season. On one occasion he and his brother Hyrum met me when on the sea going on a mission to England. I had Dan Jones with me. He received his mission from Joseph Smith before his death; and the prophet talked freely to me about the mission I was then going to perform. And he also talked to me with regard to the mission of the Twelve Apostles in the flesh, and he laid before me the work they had to perform; and he also spoke of the reward they would receive after death. And there were many other things he laid before me in his interview on that occasion. . . . I have had many interviews with Brother Joseph until the last 15 or 20 years of my life; I have not seen him for that length of time. But during my travels in the southern country last winter I had many interviews with President Young, and with Heber C. Kimball, and Geo. A. Smith, and Jedediah M. Grant, and many others who are dead. They attended our conference, they attended our meetings. And on one occasion, I saw Brother Brigham and Brother Heber ride in carriage ahead of the carriage in which I rode when I was on my way to attend conference; and they were dressed in the most priestly robes. When we arrived at our destination I asked Prest. Young if he would preach to us. He said, "No, I have finished my testimony in the flesh I shall not talk to this people any more. But (said he) I have come to see you; I have come to watch over you, and to see what the people are doing. Then (said he) I want you to teach the people—and I want you to follow this counsel yourself—that they must labor and so live as to obtain the Holy Spirit, for without this you cannot build up the kingdom; without the spirit of God you are in danger of walking in the dark, and in danger of failing to accomplish your calling as apostles and as elders in the church and kingdom of God. And, said he, Brother Joseph taught me this principle." . . . the thought came to me that Brother Joseph had left the work of watching over this church and kingdom to others, and that he had gone ahead . . .

. . . I do hope and pray God that we may magnify our calling while we tarry here, so that when we get through our earthly mission and go into the spirit world, we may meet with Brothers Joseph and Brigham and Heber and the rest of the faithful men whom we knew and labored with while in the flesh, as well as Father Adam, Enoch, Abraham, Isaac and Jacob, and all the prophets and apostles who have had their day and their time and their generation, and who have finished their work here below and gone home to glory. Do you not think they are interested about us? I tell you they are. (*Journal of Discourses*, 21:317–18.)

These were actual occurrences. They happened. President Woodruff understood the difference between actual visitations of personages, angelic visitants, and visions or other communications from God. He said, for instance, that when Paul was caught up to the third heaven and saw things not lawful to utter, not knowing whether he was in or out of the body, that was a vision. When Joseph Smith was visited by Moroni and the Apostles, he talked to them face to face. This was not a vision.

> I want to preach a short sermon to this congregation. . . .
> My mind reverts to the channels of communication from God to man. . . .
> . . . the Lord has many ways in which He communicates with us. Frequently, . . . truths, principles, warnings, etc., are communicated to the children of men by means of dreams and visions. . . .
> Then, again, there are visions. Paul, you know, on one occasion was caught up to the third heaven and saw things that were not lawful to utter. He did not know whether he was in the body or out of the body. That was a vision. When Joseph Smith, however, was visited by Moroni and the Apostles, it was not particularly a vision which he had; he talked with them face to face. (*Journal of Discourses*, 22:330–32.)

In point of fact President Woodruff did have experiences with heavenly messengers instructing him in vision. When he recorded them, he was careful to delineate the difference between a vision and a face-to-face confrontation.

> I will refer to a thing that took place with me in Tennessee. I was in Tennessee in the year 1835, and while at the house of Abraham O. Smoot, I received a letter from Brothers Joseph Smith and Oliver Cowdery, requesting me to stay there, and stating that I would lose no blessing by doing

so. Of course, I was satisfied. I went into a little room and sat down upon a small sofa. I was all by myself and the room was dark; and while I rejoiced in this letter and the promise made to me, I became wrapped in vision. I was like Paul; I did not know whether I was in the body or out of the body. A personage appeared to me and showed me the great scenes that should take place in the last days. One scene after another passed before me. I saw . . . the various dispensations of God to man. . . . I saw the resurrection of the dead. . . . What does this mean? It was a testimony of the resurrection of the dead. I had a testimony. I believe in the resurrection of the dead, and I know it is a true principle. (*Journal of Discourses*, 22:332–33.)

While we have President Wilford Woodruff before us, we shall elicit some more testimony about angels. He talked to the Saints, again as recorded in general conference, about one of the more common type of visits from the other world. It is within the author's experience, and I am convinced that it is within the experience of many of the readers and/or their families, that persons who have preceded us in death are not infrequently dispatched to us as messengers and guides. President Woodruff said:

I have felt of late as if our brethren on the other side of the [veil] had held a council, and that they had said to this one, and that one, "Cease thy work on earth, come hence, we need help," and they have called this man and that man. It has appeared so to me in seeing the many men who have been called from our midst lately. Perhaps I may be permitted to relate a circumstance with which I am acquainted in relation to Bishop Roskelley, of Smithfield, Cache Valley. On one occasion he was suddenly taken very sick—near to death's door. While he lay in this condition, President Peter Maughan, who was dead, came to him and said: "Brother Roskelley, we held a council on the other side of the [veil]. I have had a great deal to do, and I have the privilege of coming here to appoint one man to come and help. I have had three names given to me in council, and you are one of them, I want to inquire into your circumstances." The Bishop told him what he had to do, and they conversed together as one man would converse with another. President Maughan then said to him: "I think I will not call you. I think you are wanted here more than perhaps one of the others." Bishop Roskelley got well from that hour. Very soon after, the second man was taken sick, but not being able to exercise sufficient faith, Brother Roskelley did not go to him. By and by this man recovered, and on meeting Brother Roskelley he said: "Brother Maughan came to me the other night and told me he was sent to call one man from the ward," and he named two men as had been done to Brother Roskelley. A few days afterwards the third man was taken sick and died. Now, I name this to show a principle. They have work on the other side of the [veil]; and they want men, and they call them. (*Journal of Discourses*, 22:334–35.)

It is noted that this other-worldly visitation had to do with the general body of the faithful Saints, not, as President Woodruff said, those "who bear rule in Zion." Experiences with angels are reserved for the faithful, not particularly for those in administrative positions.

BRIGHAM YOUNG

For our next witness we call Brigham Young, the second president of the Church. His testimony is cumulative in nature because it had to do with an angel who was a just man made perfect. It is noted that this instance took place in the form of a night vision or dream. It was recorded in the *Manuscript History of Brigham Young* on 23 February 1847, at Winter Quarters.

While sick and asleep about noonday of the 17th inst., I dreamed that I went to see Joseph. He looked perfectly natural, sitting with his feet on the lower round of his chair. I took hold of his right hand and kissed him many times, and said to him: "Why is it that we cannot be together as we used to be[?] You have been from us a long time, and we want your society and I do not like to be separated from you."

Joseph rising from his chair and looking at me with his usual earnest, expressive and pleasing countenance replied, "It is all right."

I said, "I do not like to be away from you."

Joseph said, "It is all right; we cannot be together yet; we shall be by and by; but you will have to do without me a while, and then we shall be together again."

I then discovered there was a hand rail between us, Joseph stood by a window and to the southwest of him it was very light. I was in the twilight and to the north of me it was very dark; I said, "Brother Joseph, the brethren you know well, better than I do; you raised them up, and brought the Priesthood to us. The brethren have a great anxiety to understand the law of adoption or sealing principles; and if you have a word of counsel for me, I should be glad to receive it."

Joseph stepped toward me, and looking very earnestly, yet pleasantly said, "Tell the people to be humble and faithful, and be sure to keep the spirit of the Lord and it will lead them right. Be careful and not turn away the small still voice; it will teach you what to do and where to go; it will yield the fruits of the kingdom. Tell the brethren to keep their hearts open to conviction, so that when the Holy Ghost comes to them, their hearts will be ready to receive it. They can tell the Spirit of the Lord from all other spirits; it will whisper peace and joy to their souls; it will take malice, hatred, strife and all evil from their hearts; and their whole desire will be to do good, bring forth righteousness and build up the kingdom of God. Tell the brethren if they will follow the spirit of the Lord, they will go right. Be sure to tell the people to keep the Spirit of the Lord; and if they will, they will find themselves just as they were organized by our Father in Heaven before they came into the world. Our Father in Heaven organized the human family, but they are all disorganized and in great confusion."

Joseph then showed me the pattern, how they were in the beginning. This I cannot describe, but I saw it, and saw where the Priesthood had been taken from the earth and how it must be joined together, so that there would be a perfect chain from Father Adam to his latest posterity. Joseph again said, "Tell the people to be sure to keep the Spirit of the Lord and follow it, and it will lead them just right."

HEBER C. KIMBALL

Heber C. Kimball, paternal grandfather of President Spencer W. Kimball, served as a counselor to Brigham Young in the First Presidency of the Church. His reputation for honesty and integrity is unblemished. He was so sensitive to spiritual phenomena that President Young referred to him as his prophet. President

Kimball had much to do with angels. He recorded, for instance, " . . . we did not fear, nor hesitate to proceed on our journey, for God was with us, and angels went before us, and we had no fear of either men or devils. This we knew because they (the angels) were seen" (*Life of Heber C. Kimball*, 43–44).

It was President Kimball who recorded the name of one of the angelic ministrants who attended the dedication of the Kirtland Temple. "While these things were being attended to the beloved disciple John was seen in our midst by the Prophet Joseph, Oliver Cowdery and others" (ibid., 92). He was there and recorded the happening.

As Heber C. Kimball was being prepared for the wondrous ministry that was to be his, he was given a view of angels that was similar to Elisha's seeing the army of angels that helped fight Israel's battles. Although he did not know it at the time, the great latter-day work had begun. There was conflict and the heavens were bestirring themselves. Truth and error were pitted against each other and the invisible world was up in arms. The prophesied signs in the heavens were showing. Of the night of 22 September 1827, he wrote:

> I had retired to bed, when John P. Greene, who was living within a hundred steps of my house, came and waked me up, calling upon me to come out and behold the scenery in the heavens. I woke up and called my wife and Sister Fanny Young (sister to Brigham Young), who was living with us, and we went out-of-doors.
>
> It was one of the most beautiful starlight nights, so clear that we could see to pick up a pin. We looked to the eastern horizon, and beheld a white smoke arise toward the heavens; as it ascended it formed itself into a belt, and made a noise like the sound of a mighty wind, and continued southwest, forming a regular bow dipping in the western horizon. After the bow had formed, it began to widen out and grow clear and transparent, of a bluish cast; it grew wide enough to contain twelve men abreast.
>
> In this bow an army moved, commencing from the east and marching to the west; they continued marching until they reached the western horizon. They moved in platoons, and

walked so close that the rear ranks trod in the steps of their file leaders, until the whole bow was literally crowded with soldiers. We could distinctly see the muskets, bayonets and knapsacks of the men, who wore caps and feathers like those used by the American soldiers, in the last war with Britain; and also saw their officers with their swords and equipage, and the clashing the jingling of their implements of war, and could discover the forms and features of the men. The most profound order existed throughout the entire army; when the foremost man stepped, every man stepped at the same time; I could hear the steps. When the front rank reached the western horizon a battle ensued, as we could distinctly hear the report of arms and the rush.

No man could judge of my feelings when I beheld that army of men, as plainly as ever I saw armies of men in the flesh; it seemed as though every hair of my head was alive. This scenery we gazed upon for hours, until it began to disappear.

After I became acquainted with Mormonism, I learned that this took place the same evening that Joseph Smith received the records of the Book of Mormon from the angel Moroni, who had held those records in his possession.

John Young, Sen., and John P. Greene's wife, Rhoda, were also witnesses. (Ibid., 15–17.)

President Kimball's experiences led him to the belief that angels are daily around us. He thus wrote:

I am now in my fifty-fourth year; I am a Latter-day Saint, full in the faith, and not only in the faith, but I have a knowledge of the truth of this work. I know that God lives and dwells in the heavens; for I have asked Him scores of times, and hundreds of times, for things, and have received them. Is not that a pretty good proof that He hears me, when I ask him for things and get them; and is not that a proof that He lives, and dwells in the heavens? I think it is. I suppose He dwells there. He could not dwell anywhere else, but in what particular portion He dwells, I do not precisely know, though He is not so far off as many imagine. He is near by, His angels are our associates, they are with us and around about us, and watch over us, and take care of us, and lead us, and guide us, and administer to our wants in their ministry and in their holy calling unto which they are appointed. We are told in the Bible that angels are ministering spirits to minister to those who shall become heirs of salvation.

We have the spirits of the ancients, also, administering to the Saints:

Who have you now in your midst? Have you Abraham and Isaac and the Apostles Peter, James and John? Yes, you have them right in your midst—they are talking to you all the time.

Who are you to be subject to? You say you are willing to be subject to God—to Jesus Christ. You are willing if Peter came along to listen to him. Well, Peter is here, John is here, Elias is here, Elijah is here, Jesus is here, and the Father is here. What! In person? If not in person, their authority is here, with all the power that ever was or ever will be, to seal men and women up to everlasting. (Ibid., 460–61.)

HEBER J. GRANT

We next call Heber J. Grant, seventh president of The Church of Jesus Christ of Latter-day Saints. The author has never known a more credible witness. The experiences I have known him to relate, including this instant testimony, were told with painful accuracy. He had a reputation for never exaggerating. His recounting of an experience was known for accuracy in the most minute detail.

The remarkable experience that he tells is, once again, cumulative. Without further multiplying examples, the honest inquirer is convinced of the realness of just men made perfect and their workings with men in the flesh.

Forty years ago this October conference [1922], I met the late Elder George Teasdale at the south gate of the Tabernacle grounds. He shook hands with me and said: "Brother Grant, I am delighted to see you. You and I are going to be—" and he stopped suddenly and his face turned red. But the Lord gave me the balance of the sentence. Four times in my life I have been permitted to read the thoughts of people. The balance of Brother Teasdale's sentence was—"sustained this afternoon as apostles of the Lord Jesus Christ to fill the vacancies in the

Quorum." And that went through me like a shock of electricity.

I came to the Sunday afternoon meeting of the conference, because of this partial sentence, and the balance that was given to me, with the assurance in my heart that Brother Teasdale and myself would be sustained as apostles. Those of you who were at that conference remember that it adjourned without filling those vacancies. I do not believe that any mortal man ever more humbly supplicated God during the next few days to forgive him for his egotism than I did for thinking I was to be chosen as an apostle. As you are aware, within a week a revelation came to John Taylor calling Brother Teasdale and myself to those positions. (*Gospel Standards,* 193–94.)

President Grant also gave us this stirring testimony:

While on the Navajo Indian reservation with Brigham Young, Jr., and a number of others, six or eight on horseback, and several others in "white tops"—I was riding along with Lot Smith at the rear of that procession. Suddenly the road veered to the left almost straight, but there was a well-beaten path leading ahead. I said: "Stop, Lot, stop. Where does this trail lead? There are plenty of footmarks and plenty of horses' hoof marks here." He said, "It leads to an immense gully just a short distance ahead, that it is impossible to cross with a wagon. We have made a regular 'Muleshoe' of miles here to get on the other side of the gully."

I had visited the day before the spot where a Navajo Indian had asked George A. Smith, Jr., to let him look at his pistol. George A. handed it to him, and the Navajo shot him.

I said, "Lot, is there any danger from Indians here?"

"None at all."

"I want to be all alone. Go ahead and follow the crowd." I first asked him if I allowed the animal I was riding to walk if I would reach the road on the other side of the gully before the horsemen and the wagons, and he said, "Yes."

As I was riding along to meet them on the other side, I seemed to see, and I seemed to hear, what to me is one of the most real things in all my life. I seemed to hear the words that were spoken. I listened to the discussion with a great deal of interest. The First Presidency and the Quorum of the Twelve Apostles had not been able to agree on two men to fill the vacancies in the Quorum of the Twelve. There had been a vacancy of one for two years, and a vacancy of two for one year, and the conferences had adjourned without the vacancies' being filled. In this council the Savior was present, my father was there, and the Prophet Joseph Smith was there. They discussed the question that a mistake had been made in not filling those two vacancies and that in all probability it would be another six months before the Quorum would be completed. And they discussed as to whom they wanted to occupy those positions, and decided that the way to remedy the mistake that had been made in not filling these vacancies was to send a revelation. It was given to me that the Prophet Joseph Smith and my father mentioned me and requested that I be called to that position. I sat there and wept for joy. It was given to me that I had done nothing to entitle me to that exalted position, except that I had lived a clean, sweet life. It was given to me that because of my father's having practically sacrificed his life in what was known as the great reformation, so to speak, of the people in early days, having been practically a martyr, that the Prophet Joseph and my father desired me to have that position, and it was because of their faithful labors that I was called, and not because of anything I had done of myself or any great thing that I had accomplished. It was also given to me that that was all these men, the Prophet and my father, could do for me. From that day it depended upon me and upon me alone as to whether I made a success of my life or a failure. (Ibid., 195–96.)

I recall President Grant telling this experience in my presence. I was struck with wonder at the closeness of this prophet with those who were presiding on the other side of the veil of death. I pondered the fact that President Grant's father, who had before him served in the First Presidency, was acting as his advocate there in the heavenly councils. My memory of the incident was of his father saying, "What of the boy I raised up unto you?" To me this intimate glimpse into the world beyond is filled with hope and warmth. Certainly with President Grant there seemed to be many with him.

PARLEY P. PRATT

We now turn to another type of experience with an angel. Parley P. Pratt is the participant. The happening took place in May 1834. Our witness was a member of the first Council of the Twelve Apostles called in this dispensation.

It was now the first of May, 1834, and our mission had resulted in the assembling of about two hundred men at Kirtland, with teams, baggage, provisions, arms, etc., for a march of one thousand miles, for the purpose of carrying some supplies to the afflicted and persecuted Saints in Missouri, and to reinforce and strengthen them; and, if possible, to influence the Governor of the State to call out sufficient additional force to cooperate in restoring them to their rights. This little army was led by President Joseph Smith in person. It commenced its march about the first of May; passing through Ohio, Indiana, and Illinois, it entered Missouri some time in June.

I was chiefly engaged as a recruiting officer, and, not being much with the camp, can give but little of its history. I visited branches of the Church in Ohio, Indiana, Illinois and Missouri, and obtaining what men and means I could, fell in with the camp from time to time with additional men, arms, stores and money. On one occasion, I had travelled all night to overtake the camp with some men and means, and having breakfasted with them and changed horses, I again started ahead on express to visit other branches, and do business to again overtake them. At noon I had turned my horse loose from the carriage to feed on the grass in the midst of a broad, level plain. No habitation was near; stillness and repose reigned around me; I sank down overpowered with a deep sleep, and might have lain in a state of oblivion till the shades of night had gathered about me, so completely was I exhausted for want of sleep and rest; but I had only slept a few moments till the horse had grazed sufficiently, when a voice, more loud and shrill than I have ever before heard, fell on my ear, and thrilled through every part of my system; it said: *"Parley, it is time to be up and on your journey."* In the twinkling of an eye I was perfectly aroused; I sprang to my feet so suddenly that I could not at first recollect where I was, or what was before me to perform. I related the circumstance afterwards to brother Joseph Smith, and he bore testimony that it was the angel of

the Lord who went before the camp, who found me overpowered with sleep, and thus awoke me. (*Autobiography of Parley
Parker Pratt*, 1928, 93–94.)

DAVID O. McKAY

It is not unusual for angels to attend earthly religious meetings
and other sacred occasions. It has been authoritatively stated that
angels attended the dedication of the Kirtland Temple. Of this
occasion Joseph Smith recorded in his diary: "I bore record of . . .
the ministration of angels. . . . President David Whitmer also saw
angels in the house." He continues:

> Brother George A. Smith arose and began to prophesy,
> when a noise was heard like the sound of a rushing mighty
> wind, which filled the Temple, and all the congregation simul-
> taneously arose, being moved upon by an invisible power;
> many began to speak in tongues and prophesy; others saw
> glorious visions; and I beheld the Temple was filled with angels,
> which fact I declared to the congregation. The people of the
> neighborhood came running together (hearing an unusual
> sound within, and seeing a bright light like a pillar of fire rest-
> ing upon the Temple), and were astonished at what was taking
> place. (*History of the Church*, 2:427–28.)

Such presence of angels is sufficiently common that it is
within the relatively limited realm of experience of the author.

The witness selected to testify of this type of experience is
David O. McKay, ninth president of the Church. The specific
instance recited should be given special credence because it contains a prophecy that has since been specifically performed.

> I was on my first mission, president, at the time, of the
> Scottish conference in the year 1899. Presiding over the
> European Mission were Elders Platt D. Lyman, Henry W.
> Naisbitt, and James L. McMurrin. President McMurrin repre-
> sented the European Mission presidency at a conference held
> in Glasgow, Scotland. Following a series of meetings, we held a
> most remarkable priesthood meeting—one that will never be
> forgotten by any who was present.

I remember as if it were but yesterday, the intensity of the inspiration of that occasion. Everybody felt the rich outpouring of the Spirit of the Lord. All present were truly of one heart and one mind. Never before had I experienced such an emotion. It was a manifestation for which as a doubting youth I had secretly prayed most earnestly on hillside and in meadow. It was an assurance to me that sincere prayer is answered "sometime, somewhere."

During the progress of the meeting, an elder on his own initiative arose and said, "Brethren, there are angels in this room." Strange as it may seem, the announcement was not startling; indeed, it seemed wholly proper; though it had not occurred to me there were divine beings present. I only knew that I was overflowing with gratitude for the presence of the Holy Spirit. I was profoundly impressed, however, when President James L. McMurrin arose and confirmed that statement by pointing to one brother sitting just in front of me and saying, "Yes, brethren, there are angels in this room, and one of them is the guardian angel of that young man sitting there," and he designated one who today is a patriarch of the Church.

Pointing to another elder, he said, "And one is the guardian angel of that young man there," and he singled out one whom I had known from childhood. Tears were rolling down the cheeks of both of these missionaries, not in sorrow or grief, but as an expression of the overflowing Spirit; indeed, we were all weeping.

Such was the setting in which James L. McMurrin gave what has since proved to be a prophecy. I had learned by intimate association with him that James McMurrin was pure gold; his faith in the gospel implicit; that no truer man, no more loyal man to what he thought was right ever lived; so when he turned to me and gave what I thought then was more of a caution than a promise, his words made an indelible impression upon me. Paraphrasing the words of the Savior to Peter, he said: "Let me say to you, Brother David, Satan hath desired you that he may sift you as wheat, but God is mindful of you." Then he added, "If you will keep the faith, you will yet sit in the leading councils of the Church." (*Cherished Experiences*, 12–14.)

HAROLD B. LEE

The next witness summoned is Harold B. Lee, eleventh president of the Church. Once again we have a cautious and conservative witness. He is called to give his experience in being literally administered to by a personage from the unseen world. As with other cited testimony, his statement was voluntarily given in the solemnity of a general conference. On 8 April 1973, in the Salt Lake Tabernacle, President Lee said:

> May I impose upon you for a moment to express appreciation for something that happened to me some time ago. I was suffering from an ulcer condition that was becoming worse and worse. We had been touring a mission; my wife, Joan, and I were impressed the next morning that we should get home as quickly as possible, although we had planned to stay for some other meetings.
>
> On the way across the country, we were sitting in the forward section of the airplane. Some of our Church members were in the next section of the airplane. As we approached a certain point en route, someone laid his hand upon my head. I looked up; I could see no one. That happened again before we arrived home, again with the same experience. Who it was, by what means or what medium, I may never know, except I knew that I was receiving a blessing that I came a few hours later to know I needed most desperately.
>
> As soon as we arrived home, my wife very anxiously called the doctor. It was now about 11 o'clock at night. He called me to come to the telephone, and he asked me how I was; and I said, "Well, I am very tired. I think I will be all right." But shortly thereafter, there came massive hemorrhages which, had they occurred while we were in flight, I wouldn't be here today talking about it.
>
> I know that there are powers divine that reach out when all other help is not available. (*Stand Ye in Holy Places*, 187–88.)

President Lee knew, as did King David before him, "The angel of the Lord encampeth round about them that fear him, and delivereth them" (Psalm 34:7).

ALEXANDER NEIBAUR

As heretofore discussed, the Lord is not an angel in the usual sense. However, he does play the part of an angel and is the messenger of salvation. We now call a witness who had to do with more than one angel, as we shall see. He was ministered to by the Lord of all angels.

Alexander Neibaur was born in Ehrenbriestein, France, January 8, 1808. It was then a part of Alsace-Lorraine, but it now [is] German territory. The parents of Alexander were Nathan and Rebecca Peretz Neibaur. They were of the higher class of Hebrews. This is evidenced by the fact that the father was well educated, being a physician and surgeon, as well as a facile linguist. He intended his son Alexander for the Jewish ministry and had him educated for a rabbi to elucidate the Law of Moses; but when the boy was seventeen years old he decided that he did not wish this career, and chose the profession of a surgeon and dentist. He attended the University of Berlin, graduating before he was twenty years of age.

He set out on his travels immediately after leaving the University, and became converted to the Christian faith. He finally located for some time in the city of Preston, England, where he met and married an excellent wife, by name, Ellen Breakel. Here the couple were found on July 30, 1837, when the first "Mormon" elders came over to open the Gospel door to the British mission at the famous "Cock-pit," Preston, England.

The story of his conversion is full of interest. It was one morning very early. . . . The women of Preston . . . had the custom of going out before sunrise to give their front stone steps and porticos a coat of whitewash. . . . It was on one of these mornings that the young wife of Alexander Neibaur was on her knees polishing to the last degree of whiteness her own steps, when a neighbor challenged her attention with the remark:

"Have you seen the new ministers from America?"

"No," answered the younger woman, still intent on her work.

"Well," asserted the neighboring housewife laconically, as befits great tidings, "They claim to have seen an angel."

"What?" rang out an abrupt voice from an inner chamber, as the young Hebrew husband sprang from his couch and put his head out of the window. "What's that you say?"

The information was repeated for his benefit, and hurriedly dressing, the young man secured the address of the American preachers of this strange religion; and not many hours after he was in close conversation with Elders Heber C. Kimball, Willard Richards, Orson Hyde and Joseph Fielding. His was the swift conversion of spirit that demanded baptism on the spot. One of the first questions he asked, was, "You have a book?" And nothing could satisfy that eager, inspired question till he had a copy of the Book of Mormon in his own hands, for he had seen it, so he declared, in his night visions and recognized the Book on sight. He was waiting for the great message.

He was advised by the elders to wait and investigate further. Taking the book home with him, he read it through in three days. He said later that he could neither eat nor sleep till he had mastered all the contents of that wondrous volume. When he returned the book he offered himself for baptism, but was advised to wait till he was prepared. He answered, "Gentlemen, I am prepared." And his subsequent life found him always prepared. He accepted the counsel, however, and waited till the following spring. . . .

Brother Neibaur's wife could not see the gospel so quickly nor so easily as did her husband. He sat long evenings reading the Book of Mormon to his wife. . . .

His baptism occurred on April 9th, 1838. . . . This step was not taken without many sacrifices and trials. His new friends and former associates were indeed bitter and relentless in their opposition to the further conversion of this brilliant young Hebrew. He had made friends through his business associations as well as through the genial manner and the honest nature of his life and dealings. He was of considerable promise, and all who knew him deplored the step he had taken and tried to dissuade him from wrecking his life.

Alexander Neibaur was a Jew, and he was the first of his race to accept the Gospel. . . .

. . . When he was convinced of the mission of Jesus as a Savior, he left his father's roof-tree to become a soldier of the cross; and thus when the Gospel star shone upon his horizon, he hesitated not in following its course, though it led him across the sea, into dangers manifold, and swept from him all former friends and associates. . . .

. . . He sailed from Liverpool, Sunday, February 7, 1841, in the ship "Sheffield," under the leadership of Hiram Clark with a company of 235 Saints on board. He was a student well aware of the value of history and record keeping. He began a daily journal with the sailing of that ship in which he faithfully set down the events, both great and small of that historic voyage. . . .

Arriving in Nauvoo, Brother Neibaur was welcomed by his former friends, Heber C. Kimball, and Willard Richards. Under the hands of Willard Richards and John Taylor he was ordained to the priesthood, January 18, 1843, and ordained a seventy in 1844. He was honored with the friendship of the Prophet Joseph Smith, and was fired with the same passionate zeal for the Gospel and the fearless Latter-day Prophet which characterized the leaders and other faithful members of the Church. He had the extreme pleasure of becoming instructor to the Prophet Joseph Smith in the German and Hebrew languages, and treasured all his life the blessedness of that memory and association.

Asked by one of his daughters in later life how it was that he came to accept the Gospel, he replied that he was converted to the mission of Christ long before he ever heard a Latter-day Saint elder preach. He added that subsequently he had been visited in dreams and visions and had seen the Book of Mormon brought forth in vision; also that he had become familiar with the endowment ceremonies in the same mystic manner. On this point he once had a conversation with the Prophet Joseph Smith, and told the Prophet many things that had been manifested to him in his early youth. The prophet put his arm affectionately around Brother Neibaur's shoulder and said,

"You are indeed one of us, Brother Neibaur."

. . . He practiced his profession of dentistry when there was a chance, which was not often in that pioneer struggling community. . . .

It was while living in Nauvoo that Elder Neibaur wrote some of his best poetry. . . .

It is related by one of his daughters that one day he was singing hymns, as was his frequent custom and some question was asked of her father concerning this hymn, who repeated it for her.

"Yes," he admitted, "this was written by your humble servant." When asked why his name did not appear attached to it, he replied that he had taken the poem to Brother Parley P. Pratt, who had edited it in some places. And this small assistance caused the sensitively honest soul of Elder Neibaur to shrink from asserting his authorship. . . .

. . . When the pioneers who had been to Salt Lake Valley returned, and word went out that the first company of 1848 would make ready to move westward, the soul of Elder Neibaur was wrought up within him. . . .

When once in the Valley, Elder Neibaur shared the toils and the privations of pioneer life here. He was not fitted for hard or difficult labor, but he was industrious and he did as did his associates, made the best of all his opportunities. He did not go into debt nor was he a burden to any one. He taught his family to honor the God of the Former and Latter-day Saints. He taught them lessons of morality, of frugality, and of honesty and independence.

Elder Neibaur made the adobes for his own house which was the crude one-roomed, mud-roofed affair of those very primitive days. He added a log lean-to afterwards. Then as his fortunes mended, he later built him a good adobe house on Second South and Second East where he reared his large and industrious family.

He was the pioneer dentist of Salt Lake City, he was also the pioneer match manufacturer. . . . Elder Neibaur was also engaged each winter for some years in teaching German classes. He was himself an accomplished linguist. He spoke seven languages. . . .

Shortly before his death his son said to him,

"Father you have been telling us of your long and hard experience, and we have listened with intense affection and interest. But let me ask you, is it worth it all? Is the Gospel worth all this sacrifice?"

The glow of testimony and of truth lighted the torches in the dimming eyes of that ancient Hebrew prophet and poet and he lifted his voice in firm and lofty assurance as he said:

"Yes! Yes! and more! I have seen my Savior. I have seen the prints in his hands! I know that Jesus is the Son of God, and I know that this work is true and that Joseph Smith was a prophet of God. I would suffer it all and more, far more than I have ever suffered for that knowledge even to the laying down of my body on the plains for the wolves to devour." . . .

. . . A short time before the end, his face suddenly lit up and his countenance brightened. He cast his eyes upward as if he could see far into upper distant spaces.

"What do you see, father?" they asked. The dying man murmured clearly,

"Joseph—Hyrum—" then his weary eyes closed forever.

With the burning testimony of truth on his lips he closed his life mission, laid down his body, and his soul went to meet and mingle with the redeemed of God. . . . Of such is the kingdom of heaven. (*Utah Genealogical and Historical Magazine*, April 1914, 53–63.)

EMMA SOMERVILLE McCONKIE

To conclude this personalized account of angelic administrations, I call as the final witness my grandmother, Emma Somerville McConkie. As with Alexander Neibaur, I have selected an unknown witness to demonstrate the universality of being ministered to from the heavens. Grandmother McConkie was a ward Relief Society president in Moab, Utah, many years ago. At the time of this experience she was a widow. My father wrote this in his diary.

Mother was president of the Moab Relief Society. J_____ B_____ (a non-member who opposed the Church) had married a Mormon girl. They had several children; now they had a new baby. They were very poor and Mother was going day by day to care for the child and to take them baskets of food, etc. Mother herself was ill, and more than once was hardly able to get home after doing the work at the J_____ B_____ home.

One day she returned home especially tired and weary. She slept in her chair. She dreamed she was bathing a baby which she discovered was the Christ Child. She thought, Oh, what a great honor to thus serve the very Christ! As she held the baby in her lap, she was all but overcome. She thought, who else has actually held the Christ Child? Unspeakable joy filled her whole being. She was aflame with the glory of the

Lord. It seemed that the very marrow in her bones would melt. Her joy was so great it awakened her. As she awoke, these words were spoken to her, "Inasmuch as ye have done it unto one of the least of these my brethren, ye have done it unto me." (*Relief Society Magazine*, March 1970, 169.)

While my father was alive I went to him and to his journal to make sure I had all the facts right in the preparation of a talk I was to give at a family reunion. I wanted to recount the foregoing incident in the life of his mother. At the time of the ministration from the heavens I watered it down, saying "She seemed to hear a voice." My father corrected me, saying, "She did not seem to hear a voice. She heard a voice." And that is the way it can be in the real world. It is my opinion that Alexander Neibaur and Emma Somerville McConkie have had their souls delivered by the ultimate angel. They have learned, as the Saints have in all ages before them. "God is our refuge and strength, a very present help in trouble" (Psalm 46:1). "The angel of the Lord encampeth round about them that fear him, and delivereth them" (Psalm 34:7).

True religious history demonstrates an undeviating pattern. We have models. Where men have faith, angels minister. So unvarying is this principle that it stands forth as a test of the divinity of any organization on earth. If angels minister to a people, they are the Lord's people. If angels do not minister to people, they are not the Lord's people. This is a scriptural standard (see Moroni 7:27–38). When judging by this standard, it is not difficult to find which of all churches is true.

MISSIONARIES ARE ANGELS

As we have noted, righteous mortal men on God's errand may properly be referred to as angels. One of the earliest accounts of biblical angels is of this type.

> And there came two angels to Sodom at even; and Lot sat in the gate of Sodom: and Lot seeing them rose up to meet them; and he bowed himself with his face toward the ground;

> And he said, Behold now, my lords, turn in, I pray you, into your servant's house, and tarry all night, and wash your feet, and ye shall rise up early, and go on your ways. (Genesis 19:1–2.)

The townspeople "called unto Lot, and said unto him, Where are the men which came in to thee this night?" (Genesis 19:5). The text sounds as though these angels were mortal men. Certainly the local citizenry thought so. In his inspired rendition of this chapter, the Prophet Joseph Smith indicates that these "angels of God" "were holy men" (Inspired Version, Genesis 19:15). There are several scriptural citations to angels that are conducive to such an interpretation. Righteous mortal men may play the role of angels, and it is proper to term them angels under some circumstances.

During his earthly ministry, the Lord taught of the coming end of the world and of his coming in his glory. He told of the signs of these times, and then "they shall see the Son of man coming in the clouds of heaven with power and great glory. And he shall send his angels with a great sound of a trumpet, and they shall gather together his elect from the four winds, from one end of heaven to the other" (Matthew 24:30–31).

In a revelation given through the Prophet Joseph Smith, commencing, "Listen to the voice of Jesus Christ," we are given significant insight into the meaning of this citation. We read:

> Verily, I say unto you that ye are chosen out of the world to declare my gospel with the sound of rejoicing, as with the voice of a trump. . . .
> And ye are called to bring to pass the gathering of mine elect; for mine elect hear my voice." (D&C 29:4, 7.)

The Lord uses the same terminology in both revelations. He shall send his angels with a sound of a trumpet, and missionaries are chosen out of the world to declare his gospel with the sound of rejoicing, as with the voice of a trump. The missionaries and/or angels are called to bring to pass the gathering of the elect. Clearly the missionaries are in the role of the prophesied angels.

It is proper to say that these righteous mortal messengers are angels of God.

Those performing this service in the last days are "saying with a loud voice: Fear God and give glory to him, for the hour of his judgment is come; And worship him that made heaven, and earth, and the sea, and the fountains of waters" (D&C 133:38–39). These servants of God, the missionaries of our day, are saying the very words that John saw in his vision of the restoration when he heard the angel say, "Fear God, and give glory to him; for the hour of his judgment is come: and worship him that made heaven, and earth, and sea, and the fountains of waters" (Revelation 14:7).

In addition to discharging their angelic role, righteous mortal men who "go and preach this gospel of the kingdom" are given the promise and comfort of other-world ministering by having "mine angels round about you, to bear you up" (D&C 84:80, 88).

The Apostle Paul instructed the Hebrew Saints to "be not forgetful to entertain strangers" (Hebrews 13:2). This has always seemed to me to be a missionary function. We are to entertain and teach our Father's other children—that is, the outsiders and strangers. Paul adds meaningfully, "for thereby some have entertained angels unawares" (ibid.). I think this means at least two things: First, when we invite the stranger in to teach him the gospel, and invite the missionaries in, we indeed entertain angels. And second, when we invite the stranger in to partake of the gospel, the angels of God's presence will bear us up in this righteous endeavor. We may "entertain angels unawares" when we participate in God's purposes.

A young man tearfully told me of the fulfillment of a blessing pronounced upon his head years before. It was a patriarchal blessing given prior to his receiving his call to perform full-time missionary service. "You will envision in your mind the homes of those who are waiting to receive you. You will recognize them when you see them." The angels bore him up as this pronouncement was literally fulfilled. God's errand was both told and done, both by his ministrants.

ANGELIC HYMNS

Angels have been associated with music from the beginning. Faithful and patient Job was given a glimpse of before the world was, as he spoke of the heavenly melodies heard in the courts above at that time, "when the morning stars sang together, and all the sons of God shouted for joy" (Job 38:7). I have always imagined this as a mixed chorus with the morning stars being the preeminent and leading spirits. I am honored to number among my friends one valiant woman who was told in her patriarchal blessing that she sang in the choir, in her premortal life, when the plan of salvation was announced. Vocal and instrumental music are a part of true worship. One close to me was similarly blessed with the knowledge that a trump sounded in the heavens to announce his birth on earth. Music is given of God. It furthers his purposes; angels are intimately involved with it.

An angelic chorus from heaven heralded the birth on earth of the Son of God.

> And suddenly there was with the angel a multitude of the heavenly host praising God, and saying,
> Glory to God in the highest, and on earth peace, good will toward men.
> And it came to pass, as the angels were gone away from them into heaven, the shepherds said one to another, Let us now go even unto Bethlehem, and see this thing which is come to pass, which the Lord hath made known unto us. (Luke 2:13–15.)

Similar choirs are now being trained, the scores being composed, appropriate lyrics being written, instrumental accompaniment being prepared and rehearsed for our Lord's second coming. Inasmuch as this will be a coming in glory, one can scarcely comprehend the angelic music that will be part of this superlative event. The lyrics are of such importance that the name of one of the songs to be rendered, together with some of the words, was revealed to John in his great revelation, and he recorded them. He says they will sing "a new song" (Revelation 14:3). Modern revelation gives us the title, "the song of the Lamb" (D&C 133:56). As revealed to John, these are some of the words:

> Great and marvellous are thy works,
>   Lord God Almighty;
> Just and true are thy ways,
>   thou King of Saints.
> Who shall not fear thee, O Lord,
>   And glorify thy name?
> For thou only art holy:
> For all nations shall come
>   And worship before thee;
> For thy judgments are made manifest.
>   —Revelation 15:3–4

Resurrected Saints "shall sing the song of the Lamb." Righteous person have looked forward to singing "songs of everlasting joy" (D&C 45:71; 66:11; 101:8). In his last great sermon King Benjamin says, "I am about to go down to my grave . . . I . . . go down in peace, and my immortal spirit may join the choirs above in singing the praises of a just God" (Mosiah 2:28; see also Mormon 7:7; Revelation 14:2–3). I know at least one Latter-day Saint of whom a righteous patriarch said that he "shall compose a portion of the music to be rendered by the angelic choirs at the Second Coming."

What has this to do with us? I suggest that if we have interest in the fulfillment that these activities portend, we might commence to develop our spiritual and other talents. The Lord has said to us, in the here and now, "For my soul delighteth in the song of the heart; yea, the song of the righteous is a prayer unto me, and it shall be answered with a blessing upon their heads" (D&C 25:12). If we are interested in being "partakers of the divine nature" (2 Peter 1:4), we had better be about it.

There will be many who are accepted into these heavenly choirs. Those who have experienced, or seen vision of, such matters talk about "all the host of heaven" (1 Kings 22:19) and often themselves turn psalmist: "Praise ye him, all his angels: praise ye him, all his hosts" (Psalm 148:2). John gives us some evidence as to numbers. "And they sung a new song . . . And I beheld, and I heard the voice of many angels round about the throne . . . and the number of them was ten thousand times ten thousand, and thousands of thousands; Saying with a loud voice, Worthy is the Lamb" (Revelation 5:9, 11–12).

There are and will be great numbers of angels.

ANGELS COMING WITH CHRIST

So much for the choirs of angels that will accompany Jesus in his glorious second coming. There will be other heavenly hosts with differing assignments and purposes who will be on the Lord's errand and are properly included in a discussion on angels. They will attend Christ at his coming.

At his second coming, "the Lamb shall stand upon Mount Zion, and with him a hundred and forty-four thousand, having his Father's name written on their foreheads" (D&C 133:18). These are a part of the heavenly hosts. They are angels and they are more than angels. These are our Father's children who have achieved all that was given to them to achieve. They have the Father's name on their foreheads, signifying that they are the most advanced of all men and angels. They have progressed to godhood. They are gods, exalted personages. They are "redeemed from among men, . . . and in their mouth [is] found no guile: for they are without fault before the throne of God" (Revelation 14:4–5). These children of our Father have attained perfection. They have accomplished what Jesus behooved us all to do: "Be ye therefore perfect, even as your Father which is in heaven is perfect" (Matthew 5:48). They have done what Jesus did before them, for as a resurrected being, he had attained perfection. It is interesting to note the difference in terminology used by the Lord after he was resurrected. To the Nephites, after his resurrection, he said: "Therefore I would that ye should be perfect even as I, or your Father who is in heaven is perfect" (3 Nephi 12:48).

These personages who will attend Christ in his glory represent each of the tribes of Israel—except for some unspecified reason the tribe of Dan (see Revelation 7:2–8)—and "are high priests, ordained unto the holy order of God, to administer the everlasting gospel; for they are they who are ordained out of every nation, kindred, tongue, and people, by the angels to whom is given power over the nations of the earth, to bring as many as will come to the church of the Firstborn" (D&C 77:11). These exalted men and angels are part of "a great multitude, which no man could number" (Revelation 7:9). All of them are exalted beings and have place in the Church of the Firstborn (see Revelation 7:9–17; Hebrews 12:22–24).

To persons of spiritual discernment it would be demeaning to inquire, "What have these to do with us?"

TESTIMONY

It has been a purpose of this essay to present information about angels in a logical and well-reasoned way. However, it should be said that we are not dealing with worldly knowledge. The truth about angels does not come from persuasive argument, regardless of reason or logic. Such thinking methods lead truth seekers along the path to things spiritually discerned. Logic and reason are aids in strengthening one's spiritual assurances. Perhaps the incomparable phraseology of Paul puts it best: "For what man knoweth the things of a man, save the spirit of man which is in him? even so the things of God knoweth no man, but the Spirit of God" (1 Corinthians 2:11).

The source of one's knowledge or assurance of the truth of the Lord's work with his messengers, the angels, comes by revelation. Such personal revelation is called a testimony and is had by way of the Holy Ghost. A spiritual certitude can only be obtained in this manner. In its nature a testimony consists of knowledge that comes by revelation from God. The Lord is called *The Angel* in a blessing given by Jacob (see Genesis 48:15–16). What has been recorded in the revelations about Jesus in this sense is applicable to all the righteous and holy angels. When the mighty and prophetic John fell at the feet of an angel to worship him, the angel said to him, "See thou do it not: I am thy fellowservant, and of thy brethren that have the testimony of Jesus: worship God:

for the testimony of Jesus is the spirit of prophecy" (Revelation 19:10). The testimony of Jesus and his angels must come by the spirit of prophecy, which is received when the Holy Ghost speaks to the spirit within men. It comes when the "still small voice" is heard by the inner man. Sometimes it is accompanied by angels, as in the case of Elijah at Horeb, the mount of God (see 1 Kings 19). Receipt of a testimony is a religious experience. In association with a testimony comes the feeling of calm, unwavering certainty. Those who have it can use logic and reason in defending their positions, but it is the prompting of the Spirit, rather than the reason, upon which the true testimony rests.

Jesus and the prophets in all ages have borne testimonies, including Christ (see John 4:25–26; 10:25, 36), Job (see Job 19:25), Peter (see Matthew 16:13–20), John (see John 6:68–69), Alma (see Alma 5:45–46), and Joseph Smith (see D&C 76:22–24).

The receipt of a testimony of spiritual truths brings a concomitant responsibility to bear witness (see Mosiah 18:9; D&C 88:81). Blessings are promised the faithful who bear testimony to the world (see D&C 62:3: 84:61). Thus, I sense an obligation to share with the reader some heretofore almost unspoken intimacies.

While serving on my first full-time mission, in New England, I was favored with a companion who gave me good balance. I was descended from old Church families; he was a convert to the Church of only a year or so before his mission call. He was a product of active Protestantism: I was a product of the restoration of all things. Between the two of us we had the breadth of experience to effectively teach many people of the fulness of the gospel.

Upon returning to his home in the northwestern United States, this strong man was beset with times of struggle. He had a large family and was under the necessity of developing a business that was very demanding. All this was time consuming and energy draining, but in addition he was loaded with Church activity, for he served in a ward bishopric.

The awful thought plagued him: *Was it worth it?* Living the gospel and serving in the Church seemed to demand so much. Would the true church take from him the time he could other-wise be spending with his family? He had to know.

This good man prepared himself in fasting and prayer. He approached the Father in the name of the Son and poured out his heart.

As he slept that night he had a vision. He saw himself in a great struggle, in the midst of a huge battle, fighting with every ounce of his strength. But the terrible doubt was there. He didn't know whether he was fighting on the right side or not. Just as he was about to abandon himself to destruction, a shaft of light appeared over his head. It rested upon one of the troopers lead-ing the battle in the section in which he was engaged. He recog-nized the man. It was his missionary companion in the New England Mission so many years before. Then he heard the voice of the Spirit: "When you are on his side, you are on the right side." Calmness and certainty were his once again. The scene closed. He knew, and was given tranquillity.

Almost immediately he made preparation to represent his ward at a general conference in Salt Lake City. There he con-tacted his old companion and in loving camaraderie, around a kitchen table eating bread and milk, he related his trial and suc-cessful overcoming of the world. He wanted his missionary com-panion's family to hear it from his own lips. This is life. This is how it is. It can be made up of treasured moments—for believers.

The vision incident to this experience was repeated to another participant nearly a quarter of a century later. A sensi-tive and spiritually mature Arizona missionary who served as my assistant reported to me that as he was pondering the meaning of this experience, the eyes of his understanding were opened. He saw the same great conflict, and the same pageant was reenacted before him. However, this time he saw himself in the midst of the battle. "And the spirit said to me that exact same words," he told me.

Publication of these two personal and sacred instances is intended to apply only to matters within the realm of spiritual discernment, such as the subject matter of this discussion on angels.

The heavens, in small measure, have been opened to me. I too have a testimony of Jesus by the spirit of prophecy. His work is true. We in The Church of Jesus Christ of Latter-day Saints are engaged in it. It was implemented in our day by his angelic ministrants, just as he said it would be. I should like to add my witness to the cumulative witnesses that encompass us. The angels came to the Prophet Joseph Smith just as he said they did. What they did is inextricably concerned with our personal salvation; we could not have it without them. Our very salvation is contingent upon angels!

SCRIPTURAL REFERENCES
TO ANGELS

THE BIBLE

Genesis

3:24	Cherubims, and a flaming sword
16:7	the angel of the Lord found her
9	the angel of the Lord said unto her
10	the angel of the Lord said unto her
11	the angel of the Lord said unto her
19:1	there came two angels to Sodom
15	then the angels hastened Lot
21:17	the angel of God called to Hagar
22:11	the angel of the Lord called unto him
15	angel of the Lord called unto Abraham
24:7	he shall send his angel before thee
40	will send his angel with thee
28:12	the angels of God ascending and descending
31:11	the angel of God spake unto me
32:1	the angels of God met him
48:16	the Angel which redeemed me

Exodus

3:2	the angel of the Lord appeared unto him
14:19	the angel of God, which went before
23:20	Behold, I send an Angel before thee
23	For mine Angel shall go before thee
25:18–20	cherubs

32:34	mine Angel shall go before thee
33:2	I will send an angel before thee
37:7–9	cherubs
Numbers	
20:16	he heard our voice, and sent an angel
22:22	the angel of the Lord stood in the way
23	the ass saw the angel of the Lord
24	the angel of the Lord stood in a path
25	when the ass saw the angel of the Lord
26	the angel of the Lord went further
27	when the ass saw the angel of the Lord
31	he saw the angel of the Lord
32	the angel of the Lord said unto him
34	Balaam said unto the angel of the Lord
35	the angel of the Lord said unto Balaam
Judges	
2:1	an angel of the Lord came up
4	when the angel of the Lord spake
5:23	Meroz, said the angel of the Lord
6:11	there came an angel of the Lord
12	angel of the Lord appeared unto him
20	the angel of God said unto him
21	the angel of the Lord put forth
21	the angel of the Lord departed
22	Gideon perceived that he was an angel
22	I have seen an angel of the Lord
13:3	the angel of the Lord appeared
6	like the countenance of an angel
9	the angel of God came again
13	the angel of the Lord said unto Manoah
15	Manoah said unto the angel of the Lord
16	the angel of the Lord said unto Manoah
16	Manoah knew not that he was an angel
17	Manoah said unto the angel of the Lord
18	And the angel of the Lord said
19	and the angel did wondrously
20	the angel of the Lord ascended in the
21	the angel of the Lord did no more appear

21	Manoah knew that he was an angel
1 Samuel	
4:4	dwelleth between the cherubims
29:9	good in my sight, as an angel of God
2 Samuel	
14:17	angel of God, so is my lord the king
20	according to the wisdom of an angel of God
19:27	the king is as an angel of God
22:11	And he rode upon a cherub
24:16	when the angel stretched out his hand
16	said to the angel that destroyed
16	angel of the Lord was by the threshingplace
17	the angel that smote the people
1 Kings	
6:23–29	cherubs
32, 35	cherubs
13:18	an angel spake unto me by the word
19:5	an angel touched him, and said unto
7	the angel of the Lord came again the second time
2 Kings	
1:3	the angel of the Lord said to Elijah
15	the angel of the Lord said unto Elijah
19:35	the angel of the Lord went out
1 Chronicles	
21:12	the angel of the Lord destroying
15	God sent an angel unto Jerusalem
15	angel that destroyed
15	And the angel of the Lord stood by
16	saw the angel of the Lord
18	the angel of the Lord commanded Gad
20	Ornan turned back, and saw the angel
27	And the Lord commanded the angel
30	the sword of the angel of the Lord
2 Chronicles	
3:14	cherubs
32:21	And the Lord sent an angel

Job
4:18	his angels he charged with folly
38:7	When the morning stars sang together, and all the sons of God shouted for joy?

Psalms
8:5	thou hast made him a little lower than the angels
18:10	And he rode upon a cherub
34:7	The angel of the Lord encampeth
35:5	let the angel of the Lord chase them
6	let the angel of the Lord persecute them
55:18	for there were many with me
68:17	even thousands of angels
78:25	Man did eat angels' food
49	sending evil angels among them
80:1	thou that dwellest between the cherubims
91:11	he shall give his angels charge over thee
103:20	Bless the Lord, ye his angels
104:4	Who maketh his angels spirits
148:2	Praise ye him, all his angels

Ecclesiastes
5:6	neither say thou before the angel

Isaiah
6:2, 6	seraphims
37:36	the angel of the Lord went forth
63:9	the angel of his presence saved them

Ezekiel
10	cherubs

Daniel
3:28	who hath sent his angel
6:22	My God hath sent his angel
8:15–16	angel Gabriel as a man

Hosea
12:4	he had power over the angel

Zechariah
1:9	the angel that talked with me
11	they answered the angel of the Lord
12	angel of the Lord answered and said

13	the Lord answered the angel
14	the angel that communed with me
19	I said unto the angel
2:3	angel that talked with me went forth
3	another angel went out
3:1	standing before the angel of the Lord
3	stood before the angel
5	And the angel of the Lord stood by
6	the angel of the Lord protested
4:1	the angel that talked with me came again
4	I answered and spake to the angel
5	the angel that talked with me answered
5:5	the angel that talked with me went forth
10	said I to the angel that talked with me
6:4	I answered and said unto the angel
5	the angel answered and said unto me
12:8	the angel of the Lord before them

Matthew

1:20	the angel of the Lord appeared unto him
24	did as the angel of the Lord had bidden
2:13	angel of the Lord appeareth to Joseph
19	an angel of the Lord appeareth in a dream
28:2	the angel of the Lord descended from heaven
4:6	He shall give his angels charge concerning thee
11	angels came and ministered unto him
5	the angel answered and said unto the women
13:39	the reapers are the angels
41	The Son of man shall send forth his angels
49	the angels shall come forth
16:27	the glory of his Father with his angels
18:10	in heaven their angels do always behold
22:30	are as the angels of God in heaven
24:31	he shall send his angels
36	no, not the angels of heaven
25:31	all the holy angels with him
41	prepared for the devil and his angels
26:53	more than twelve legions of angels

Mark

1:13	the angels ministered unto him
8:38	glory of his Father with the holy angels
12:25	but are as the angels which are in heaven
13:27	then shall he send his angels
32	no, not the angels which are in heaven

Luke

1:11	appeared unto him an angel of the Lord
13	the angel said unto him, Fear not
18	Zacharias said unto the angel
19	the angel answering said unto him
26	the angel Gabriel was sent from God
28	And the angel came in unto her
30	angel said unto her, Fear not, Mary
34	Then said Mary unto the angel
35	the angel answered and said unto her
38	And the angel departed from her
2:9	the angel of the Lord came upon them
10	the angel said unto them, Fear not
13	And suddenly there was with the angel
13	a multitude of the heavenly host
15	as the angels were gone away from them
21	which was so named of the angel
4:10	He shall give his angels charge over thee
9:26	in his Father's, and of the holy angels
12:8	confess before the angels of God
9	shall be denied before the angels of God
15:10	there is joy in the presence of the angels
16:22	carried by the angels into Abraham's
20:36	for they are equal unto the angels
24:23	they had also seen a vision of angels
22:43	there appeared an angel unto him

John

1:51	the angels of God ascending and descending
5:4	angel went down at a certain season
12:29	An angel spake to him
20:12	seeth two angels in white sitting

Acts

5:19	the angel of the Lord by night
6:15	as it had been the face of an angel
7:30	an angel of the Lord in a flame of fire
35	a deliverer by the hand of the angel
38	in the wilderness with the angel
53	the law by the disposition of angels
8:26	angel of the Lord spake unto Philip
10:3	an angel of God coming in to him
7	the angel which spake unto Cornelius
22	was warned from God by an holy angel
11:13	he had seen an angel in his house
12:7	the angel of the Lord came upon him
8	the angel said unto him, Gird thyself
9	which was done by the angel
10	the angel departed from him
11	the Lord hath sent his angel
15	said they, It is his angel
23	the angel of the Lord smote him
23:8	no resurrection, neither angel, nor spirit
9	if a spirit or an angel hath spoken
27:23	there stood by me this night the angel

1 Corinthians

4:9	unto the world, and to angels, and to men
6:3	Know ye not that we shall judge angels?
11:10	power on her head because of the angels
13:1	speak with the tongues of men and of angels

2 Corinthians

11:14	is transformed into an angel of light

Galatians

1:8	we, or an angel from heaven, preach
3:19	it was ordained by angels
4:14	received me as an angel of God

Colossians

2:18	humility and worshipping of angels

2 Thessalonians

1:7	from heaven with his mighty angels

1 Timothy
3:16   justified in the Spirit, seen of angels
5:21   Jesus Christ, and the elect angels

Hebrews
1:4   made so much better than the angels
5   unto which of the angels said he at any time
6   let all the angels of God worship him
7   of the angels he saith
7   Who maketh his angels spirits
13   to which of the angels said he at any time
2:2   if the word spoken by angels
5   unto the angels hath he not put
7   a little lower than the angels
9   made a little lower than the angels
16   he took not on him the nature of angels
9:5   over it the cherubims
12:22   an innumerable company of angels
13:2   some have entertained angels unawares

1 Peter
1:12   which things the angels desire to look into
3:22   angels and authorities and powers

2 Peter
2:4   God spared not the angels that sinned
11   angels, which are greater in power

Jude
6   the angels which kept not their first estate

Revelation
1:1   signified it by his angel
20   the angels of the seven churches
2:1   Unto the angel of the church of Ephesus
8   unto the angel of the church in Smyrna
12   to the angel of the church in Pergamos
18   unto the angel of the church in Thyatira
3:1   unto the angel of the church in Sardis
5   before my Father, and before his angels
7   to the angel of the church in Philadelphia
14   unto the angel of the church of the Laodiceans
5:2   I saw a strong angel proclaiming

11	I heard the voice of many angels
7:1	I saw four angels standing on the four corners
2	cried with a loud voice to the four angels
2	I saw another angel ascending from the east
11	all the angels stood round about the throne
8:2	I saw the seven angels which stood before God
3	another angel came and stood at the altar
4	ascended up before God out of the angel's hand
5	the angel took the censer, and filled it
6	the seven angels which had the seven trumpets
7	The first angel sounded
8	the second angel sounded
10	the third angel sounded
12	the fourth angel sounded
13	an angel flying through the midst of heaven
13	voices of the trumpet of the three angels
9:1	the fifth angel sounded
11	which is the angel of the bottomless pit
13	And the sixth angel sounded
14	Saying to the sixth angel which had the trumpet
14	Loose the four angels which are bound
15	And the four angels were loosed
10:1	And I saw another mighty angel
5	the angel which I saw stand upon the sea
7	of the voice of the seventh angel
8	which is open in the hand of the angel
9	I went unto the angel
10	I took the little book out of the angel's hand
11:1	and the angel stood, saying, Rise
15	the seventh angel sounded
12:7	angels fought against the dragon
7	the dragon fought and his angels
9	his angels were cast out with him
14:6	I saw another angel fly in the midst
8	And there followed another angel
9	the third angel followed them
10	in the presence of the holy angels

15	another angel came out of the temple
17	another angel came out of the temple
19	the angel thrust in his sickle into the earth
15:1	seven angels having the seven last plagues
6	seven angels came out of the temple
7	gave unto the seven angels seven golden vials
8	seven plagues of the seven angels
16:1	saying to the seven angels
3	the second angel poured out his vial
4	the third angel poured out his vial
5	I heard the angel of the waters say
8	the fourth angel poured out his vial
10	the fifth angel poured out his vial
12	the sixth angel poured out his vial
17	the seventh angel poured out his vial
17:1	there came one of the seven angels
7	And the angel said unto me
18:1	I saw another angel come down from heaven
21	a mighty angel took up a stone
19:17	I saw an angel standing in the sun
20:1	I saw an angel come down from heaven
21:9	there came unto me one of the seven angels
12	and at the gates twelve angels
17	the measure of a man, that is, of the angel
22:6	his angel to shew unto his servants
8	before the feet of the angel
16	have sent mine angel to testify

THE BOOK OF MORMON

1 Nephi

1:8	numberless concourses of angels

2 Nephi

4:24	angels came down and ministered unto me
9:8	angel who fell from before the presence of the Eternal God
9	we become devils, angels to a devil

THE DOCTRINE AND COVENANTS

2:1–3	(Words spoken by Moroni, the angel, to Joseph Smith)
7:6	I will make him as flaming fire and a ministering angel
13	the keys of the ministering of angels
20:6	God ministered unto him by an holy angel
10	confirmed to others by the ministering of angels
27	(A holy angel speaks to Joseph Smith)
35	the ministering of angels
27:16	I have sent mine angels to commit unto you
29:28	prepared for the devil and his angels
37	and thus came the devil and his angels
42	I, the Lord God, should send forth angels
38:1	all the seraphic hosts of heaven
12	angels are waiting the great command
42:6	declaring my word like unto angels of God
43:25	and by the ministering of angels
45:44	with all the holy angels
45	an angel shall sound his trump
49:7	no man knoweth, neither the angels in heaven
23	the angel shall sound his trumpet
62:3	recorded in heaven for the angels to look upon
63:54	will I send mine angels to pluck out the wicked
67:13	neither the ministering of angels
76:21	And saw the holy angels
25	an angel of God who was in authority
33	with the devil and his angels in eternity
36	brimstone, with the devil and his angels
44	with the devil and his angels in eternity
67	an innumerable company of angels
88	telestial receive it of the administering of angels
77:8	they are four angels sent forth from God
9	the angel ascending from the east
9	he crieth unto the four angels
11	by the angels to whom is given power

12	the sounding of the trumpets of the seven angels
84:26	key of the ministering of angels
28	was ordained by the angel of God
42	mine angels charge concerning you
88	angels round about you, to bear you up
86:5	the angels are crying unto the Lord
88:2	the angels rejoice over you
92	angels shall fly through the midst of heaven
98	the sounding of the trump of the angel of God
103	the fifth angel who committeth the everlasting gospel
105	another angel shall sound his trump
106	another angel shall sound his trump
107	then shall the angels be crowned
108	the first angel again sound his trump
109	the second angel sound his trump
110	the seventh angel shall sound his trump
112	And Michael, the seventh angel
89:21	the destroying angel shall pass by them
90:34	the angels rejoice over them
103:19	Mine angel shall go up before you
20	Mine angels shall go up before you
107:20	keys of the ministering of angels
109:22	thine angels have charge over them
79	bright, shining seraphs around thy throne
110:11–16	(Moses, Elias, Elijah visit Joseph Smith and Oliver Cowdery)
121:27	pointed to by the angels
123:7	we owe to God, to angels
128:20	Moroni, an angel from heaven
20	he appeared as an angel of light
20	(Peter, James, and John talk to Joseph Smith)
21	divers angels, from Michael or Adam down to the present
21	the voice of Michael, the archangel; the voice of Gabriel, and of Raphael, and of divers angels,

THE PEARL OF GREAT PRICE

BIBLIOGRAPHY

SCRIPTURES AND BOOKS

Apocrypha.

Bible, King James Version.

Bible, Inspired Version.

Book of Mormon.

Doctrine and Covenants.

Pearl of Great Price.

Bluth, John V. *Concordance to the Doctrine and Covenants*. Salt Lake City: Deseret Book Co., 1973.

Clark, J. Reuben, Jr. *On the Way to Immortality and Eternal Life*. Salt Lake City: Deseret Book Co., 1949.

Cowley, Matthias F. *Wilford Woodruff, History of His Life and Labors*. Salt Lake City: Bookcraft, 1964.

Grant, Heber J. *Gospel Standards*. Compiled by G. Homer Durham. Salt Lake City: Improvement Era, 1969.

Journal of Discourses. 26 vols. Liverpool, England, 1862; Photo Lithographic Reprint, Los Angeles, 1961. (Abbreviated *JD*.)

Lee, Harold B. *Ye Are the Light of the World*. Salt Lake City: Deseret Book Co., 1974.

————. *Stand Ye in Holy Places*. Salt Lake City: Deseret Book Co., 1974.

McConkie, Bruce R. *Doctrinal New Testament Commentary*. Vol. 3. Salt Lake City: Bookcraft, 1973.

————. *Mormon Doctrine*. 2d. ed. Salt Lake City: Bookcraft, 1966.

McKay, David O. *Cherished Experiences*. Compiled by Clare Middlemiss. Salt Lake City: Deseret Book Co., 1965.

Pratt, Parley Parker. *Autobiography of Parley Parker Pratt*. 3d ed. Edited by Parley P. Pratt. Salt Lake City: Deseret Book Co., 1938.

Sjodahl, Janne M., and Hyrum M. Smith. *Doctrine and Covenants Commentary*. Rev. ed. Salt Lake City: Deseret Book Co., 1950.

Smith, Joseph. *History of the Church*. 7 vols. plus index. Salt Lake City: Deseret Book Co., 1951.

————. *Lectures on Faith*. Salt Lake City: Deseret Sunday School Union, 1913.

————. *Teachings of the Prophet Joseph Smith*. Compiled by Joseph Fielding Smith. Salt Lake City: Deseret Book Co., 1938. (Abbreviated *TPJS*.)

Smith, Joseph F. *Gospel Doctrine*. Salt Lake City: Deseret Book Co., 1939.

Smith, Joseph Fielding. *Doctrines of Salvation*. 3 vols. Compiled by Bruce R. McConkie. Salt Lake City: Bookcraft, 1954.

Strong, James. *The Exhaustive Concordance of the Bible*. New York: Abingdon Press, 1963.

Talmage, James E. *Articles of Faith*. Salt Lake City: Deseret Book Co., 1966.

————. *Jesus the Christ*. Salt Lake City: Deseret Book Co., 1972.

————. *The Great Apostasy*. Salt Lake City: Deseret Book Co., 1964.

Watson, Elden Jay. *Manuscript History of Brigham Young*. Salt Lake City, Utah, 1968.

Webster's Seventh New Collegiate Dictionary. Springfield, Mass.: G. & C. Merriam Co., 1973.

Whitney, Orson F. *Life of Heber C. Kimball*. Salt Lake City: Bookcraft, 1967.

Woodruff, Wilford. *The Discourses of Wilford Woodruff*. Compiled by G. Homer Durham. Salt Lake City: Bookcraft, 1946.

Young, Brigham. *Discourses of Brigham Young.* Compiled by John
A. Widtsoe. Salt Lake City: Deseret Book Co., 1956.

PERIODICALS

Conference Reports. Proceedings of the annual and semiannual
general conferences of The Church of Jesus Christ of Latter-
day Saints.

Relief Society Magazine. Published by the general board of the
Relief Society, The Church of Jesus Christ of Latter-day Saints,
Salt Lake City, Utah.

Utah Genealogical and Historical Magazine. Salt Lake City, Utah.

MISCELLANEOUS

Personal correspondence with Elder Bruce R. McConkie of the
Council of the Twelve Apostles, The Church of Jesus Christ
of Latter-day Saints.

INDEX